Bel-Air
SUPPER CLUB · MOTEL
GREEN LAKE, WIS. 54941

At Random
MILWAUKEE

RESTAURANT
COCKTAILS

Sunset Supper Club
FOND DU LAC, WISCONSIN

ke Michigan, 5 miles north of Racine

COCKTAILS · ORGAN MUSIC

The Supper Club

CONNIE'S SUPPER CLUB
Hurley, Wisconsin
CLOSE COVER BEFORE STRIKING

Eve's Supper Club

Justo's Club
CLOSE COVER
BEFORE STRIKING

Yard 4 SUPPER CLUB
HY. 12 - EAU CLAIRE, WIS.
(2 blks. from the crossroads)
CLOSE COVER BEFORE STRIKING

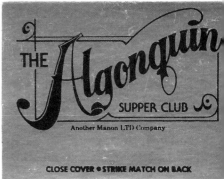

THE Algonquin SUPPER CLUB
Another Manon LTD Company
CLOSE COVER · STRIKE MATCH ON BACK

way
lub

N,
N

Lehman's
SUPPER CLUB
COCKTAILS

High Cliff
SUPPER CLUB

Food &
Cocktails
to Crow
About

THE

Wisconsin

SUPPER CLUBS

STORY

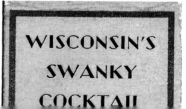

THE Wisconsin SUPPER CLUBS STORY

AN ILLUSTRATED HISTORY, WITH RELISH

RON FAIOLA

A MIDWAY BOOK

AGATE

CHICAGO

First printed in November 2021

Printed in China

10 9 8 7 6 5 4 3 2   23 24 25 26 27 28

ISBN-13: 978-1-57284-303-5
ISBN-10: 1-57284-303-9
eISBN-13: 978-1-57284-854-2
eISBN-10: 1-57284-854-5

Book design by Morgan Krehbiel
Photos by Ron Faiola, images not credited are from author's collection or as noted.

Library of Congress Cataloging-in-Publication Data is available from the Library of Congress.

Midway is an imprint of Agate Publishing. Agate books are available in bulk at discount prices. Agatepublishing.com.

To Emi and Kato

OLD-FASHIONED:

Muddle 2 dashes bitters and 1 lump sugar in Old-Fashioned glass. Add 2 ice cubes, slice of orange, twist of lemon peel. Add 1½ oz. whiskey, stir.

WHISKEY SOUR:

Shake together 2 oz. whiskey, 1 tsp. sugar and juice of ½ lemon. Strain and serve in delmonico glass with slice of orange. The sour may be made with brandy, bourbon, scotch, rye, gin or rum.

SCOTCH-ON-THE-ROCKS

Put ice cubes in Old-Fashioned glass and pour in 1½-2½ oz. scotch whisky. Serve with a twist of lemon peel.

SHERRY FLIP

Shake with ice 1 egg, 1 tsp. granulated sugar and 2 oz. sherry. Strain into delmonico glass and dust with grated nutmeg.

CHAMPAGNE COCKTAIL

In champagne glass saturate lump of sugar with bitters and dash of creme de menthe. Add 1 ice cube and twist of lemon peel. Fill glass with chilled champagne.

JACK ROSE

Shake together 1½ oz. applejack brandy, ½ oz. grenadine, juice ½ lemon with cracked ice and strain into stemmed cocktail glass.

MANHATTAN

Into a mixing glass put dash of bitters, ⅔ rye and ⅓ sweet vermouth. Mix with cracked ice, strain and serve with maraschino cherry. For a *Rob Roy* cocktail substitute scotch for rye.

STINGER

Shake with cracked ice 1 oz. white creme de menthe and 1½ oz. brandy. Strain into a stemmed cocktail glass.

MARTINI:

Fill martini pitcher with cracked ice. Pour in gin and dry vermouth in ratio of from 3-to-1 to 10-to-1. Strain, serve with an olive, with a twist of lemon peel, or for a *Gibson*, with a pearl onion.

DAIQUIRI

Shake well juice of ½ lime, 1½ oz. rum, and 1 tsp. granulated sugar with finely shaved ice and strain into sugar-rinsed glass.

Contents

STREET SCENE   MILWAUKEE, WIS.   J-492

Introduction

During the heyday of the supper club in the 1950s and 1960s, when dressing up to go out was the norm—before "come as you are" was taken too literally by some—supper clubs were seemingly everywhere, from small towns to big cities across the US, Canada, and even Europe, Australia, and Japan. In the US, they were a reflection of post-war affluence, celebrated with cocktails and fine dining. The words SUPPER CLUB on a restaurant's shingle were a beacon for those who sought an entertaining night out that might last until the wee hours. The food at supper clubs, generally referred to as American cuisine, consisted of simple, straightforward dishes that didn't require the rich sauces found in French cooking. Cocktails were the star of the show. Old-fashioneds, martinis, and Manhattans led the pack of fizzes, sours, punches, slings, rickeys, and stingers. Beer was served at saloons, and wine was for the fancy-schmancy places not everyone was able to afford. Supper clubs were like adult playgrounds back then, where cigarette smoke hung in the air and ice cream was meant to be combined with plenty of alcohol. It was grand.

Grier's Supper Club, Palatine, Illinois, 1959

The story of how supper clubs came to be is quite fascinating. For starters, they didn't just happen overnight; it took decades of fits and starts and the general public's waning morality, assisted by the Eighteenth Amendment. Looking back now, it's hard to believe that supper clubs did not originate in Wisconsin, nor Beverly Hills, as legend suggests, but somewhere else that may come as a surprise.

Among supper clubs, those in Wisconsin have always had a unique character—whether they were casual, upscale, or something in-between. Reputations were built by word of mouth and helped immensely by a recommendation from Duncan Hines (that's right, the cake mix guy—more about him later). By the 1970s, the heyday of the supper club began to diminish, as a night out for dinner was slowly transformed by sports bars, chef-centric destinations, fast-casual chains, family-friendly restaurants, and a bevy of international cuisines. The old favorites were still around but slowly fading away, often from neglect or misfortune.

This book is a tribute to the hard work and dedication—the sheer moxie—that so many supper club owners and their families must have to be a success. The stories in this book show the trials and tribulations that tested the mettle of the club owners so many years ago. The fond memories they helped create for their customers will live on.

In that regard, I must mention my personal connection to some of the establishments mentioned here, including the Rafters in Oak Creek, which was a family favorite for years. Starship, a Milwaukee punk rock club I used to frequent in the early 1980s, which hosted the likes of Lydia Lunch, Captain Beefheart, and a guitarist named Snakefinger, was also the location of two separate supper clubs, each well-known in their day.

Relish the history in these pages and keep enjoying supper clubs, where comfort food is always on the menu.

—Ron Faiola, December, 2020

(Left to right)
The Mainliner Nite Club, Des Moines, Iowa, 1945; Nicky Blair's Carnival, New York City, 1947

(Left to right)
The author's grandparents, Marie and Clark Shafer, at the Lido Cabaret, Paris, 1959; Mangam's Chateau, circa 1950s, Lyons, Illinois; Empire Room, Hotel Schroeder, Milwaukee, 1956

Chapter 1

A MILWAUKEE NATIVE IN BEVERLY HILLS

A cursory internet search for the history of supper clubs leads to more questions than answers. On the Wisconsin Historical Society's website, one can read that the first American supper club was established in the 1920s in Beverly Hills, California, by a Milwaukee native named Lawrence Frank. The article was referenced by a food blogger, repeated on Wikipedia, and therefore became "fact," like so many contemporary legends. Anyone who knows much about supper clubs will wonder how a gentleman from Milwaukee ended up opening a supper club in Beverly Hills.

Tam O'Shanter Inn,
Los Angeles, 1925

5

COURTESY OF LAWRY'S

Lawrence's story begins in the early 1800s. His grandfather, Louis Frank, ran a Milwaukee butcher shop that specialized in homemade sausages. Louis married Rosa Sternberg, and in 1847 they had a son, Nathan, who also became a butcher. Nathan eventually married Bertha Adler. Their son, Lawrence L. Frank, was born in Milwaukee in 1887.

Like with many family enterprises, the plan was for Lawrence to inherit the business and continue in the sausage trade. However, at age twenty-five, Lawrence moved to California to "get away from his uncles in the meatpacking business." It helped that Lawrence's older brother Ralph already lived in Los Angeles and ran a successful enterprise selling potato chips to hotels and restaurants.

By 1915, Lawrence had established himself in Pasadena as a furniture salesman. He sent word to his girlfriend, Henrietta "Nettie" Van de Kamp, who still lived in Milwaukee, to join him in California so they could marry. She brought her younger brother Theodore along, and soon after, Lawrence quit the furniture business to partner with Theodore selling Ralph's potato chips.

Their business, Van de Kamp Saratoga Chips, was located in downtown Los Angeles. They sold the freshly cooked chips from a walk-up window and eventually opened several more chip shops in the area. A potato shortage in 1916 caused them to expand their offerings to baked goods, and Van de Kamp's Holland Dutch Bakers was born. Lawrence's father-in-law, Henry Van de Kamp, moved to Pasadena with his wife, Sophia, and in 1920, they purchased a plot of land near Griffith Park, on what was then Tropico Avenue, and later renamed Los Feliz Boulevard. It sat vacant for a couple of years until Lawrence offered to build a small roadside coffeehouse and diner on the property.

The diner opened in 1922 as Montgomery's Country Inn run by Lawrence, his brother-in-law Walter Van de Kamp (Theodore's older brother), and Joe F. Montgomery. The menu featured fried chicken and waffle dinners, "farmer-style" frankfurters, and ham sandwiches. The building had a unique ramshackle look designed by Hollywood set decorator Harry Oliver, who also designed the Dutch-themed windmill for the Van de Kamp bakeries, which later became known for their line of frozen fish sticks.

By 1923, Lawrence Frank's brother Ralph had joined the trio, and the diner was expanded. The name was changed to

Enjoy the Fresh Food at the Most Attractive Highway Inn in Southern California

At Tropico Boulevard (popularly known as Los Feliz) and Boyce Avenue —a half mile east of Griffith Park.

IN OFFERING you fresh and wholesome country food of the highest quality obtainable, Montgomery's Country Inn fills a real need.

Here, amid quiet country surroundings—away from traffic congestion, yet within a short ride from the most exclusive residential districts—you may stop for an afternoon tea or for a country-style dinner in the dining room; for sandwiches and beverages served on the porch, at the lunch counter, *or in your car;* for Montgomery's Farmer-Style Frankfurters; or for choice fruits and vegetables.

Every detail of the service conforms to the strictest ideals of quality. The hams used for the champagne baked ham sandwiches (to take a single example), are personally selected by Mr. J. F. Montgomery—*and only the tender inner hearts of the hams are used.* Montgomery's Country-style Frankfurters, used in the frankfurter sandwiches, and sold in boxes, are recognized as the choicest grade to be secured. They are made from select pure pork and veal. Van de Kamp's Bread, known for supreme quality, is used exclusively. The hot potato salad is from Mother Montgomery's own recipe—a most appetizing dish.

The kitchen is a picture of cleanliness. Here you find plenty of sunlight; rows of shining utensils, glistening silverware, snow-white china—and the mouth-watering odor of good foods being prepared with the purest ingredients. The cuisine is under the supervision of Mr. C. Robert Peach, for several years with the famous Harvey System, whose expert guidance is responsible for the delightful country dishes that make up the Montgomery menu.

Picnic Lunch Boxes Prepared

Preparing picnic lunches involves a great deal of fuss and worry which may be avoided through the service we render.

You simply notify us in advance, describing your requirements, and the time of your arrival, and your lunch package—filled with the highest-grade foods—will be ready for you to pick up at the appointed time.

In this way, you are always certain of obtaining the freshest possible food, well prepared and neatly packed, any day during the week.

Standard boxes, containing individual picnic lunches may be secured for 50c, 75c or $1.00. Ask about them.

Montgomery's Farmer-Style Frankfurters are unsurpassed for wholesomeness and flavor

Advertisement, Montgomery's Country Inn, 1922; "Deluxe" drive-in service, circa 1930s
COURTESY OF LAWRY'S

Montgomery's Chanticleer Inn and changed again in 1925 to the Tam O'Shanter, a name inspired by a poem by Robert Burns. The Scottish-themed Tam O'Shanter was known for its hamburgers and a fifteen-cent "Milwaukee Frankfurter"—likely a nod to the Frank family's business back home. The Tam O'Shanter had outdoor seating and drive-in service—one of the first in the country at the time—which used custom-designed wooden trays for dining in cars.

The Tam O'Shanter became a popular stop for many, including Hollywood celebrities Douglas Fairbanks, Fatty Arbuckle, Mary Pickford, Gloria Swanson, and Walt Disney, whose fledgling studio and home were nearby.

With the Tam doing well, Frank had a new idea for a fine dining restaurant, inspired by the legendary London establishment Simpson's In The Strand, where meat was carved tableside from silver-domed trolleys. In 1938, he and his business partner, Walter Van de Kamp, opened Lawry's The Prime Rib on La Cienega Boulevard in Beverly Hills. As the name suggests, Lawry's menu was focused solely on one dish: prime rib, carved tableside, from a 600-pound stainless steel cart, and served with Yorkshire pudding, mashed potatoes, and a green salad. The meal cost $1.25.

While it's true that Lawry's became world-famous for its unique approach to fine dining and later for its line of seasoning salt and marinades, it's clear that some of the facts were mixed up over the years. The ham and eggs diner Lawrence Frank opened in the 1920s was definitely not a supper club. As to the question of whether Lawry's The Prime Rib was the first supper club—it was not. In fact, supper clubs were already well established long before Lawrence Frank served up his first delicious cut of prime rib in Beverly Hills.

COURTESY OF LAWRY'S

SIMPSON'S IN THE STRAND
The Famous Old English Dining House.

Telephone Nos.
4333
and
4334
Gerrard.

Telegraphic
Address:
"SIMPSONS,
STRAND,
LONDON."

VETERAN CARVERS AND SUPERINTENDENTS AT SIMPSON'S.
(The youngest of them has served there for over a quarter of a century.)
OPEN ON SUNDAYS FOR DINNERS FROM 6.0 P.M.

Manager, N. WHEELER.

Cocktails

ICE BOWL—Hearts of Irish Celery and Jumbo Ripe Olives	
Jumbo Queen Olives	35
All Fresh Fruit Cocktail	25
Snappy Tomato Cocktail a la Lawry	25
Tomato Juice	20
Filet of Marinated Herring	20
Alaska Shrimp Cocktail	35
Lobster Cocktail	45
Crab Flake Cocktail	50
Volga Beluga Caviar Canape	1.00

Salads

Chef's Salad Bowl	
With Chicken	50
With Alaska Shrimp	75
With Crab Flake	65
With Roquefort Cheese	75
All Fresh Fruit Salad, cream dressing	65
Fresh Hawaiian Pineapple and Cottage Cheese	65
Hearts of Lettuce	60
Lettuce and Tomatoes	25
Crab, Shrimp or Lobster Louie	35
Chicken Salad, a la Lawry	75
Choice of dressings	75

Features

SPAGHETTI a la Lawry	60
Italian Spaghetti, Fresh Tomatoes, Mushrooms. Meat Sauce. Cooked to order; allow 10 minutes.	
Casserole of SPAGHETTI BOLOGNAISE	75
Consisting of Meat Balls, Mushrooms, Cepes and grated Parmesan Cheese. (Cooked to order, allow 10 minutes.)	
BROILED VIRGINIA HAM or CANADIENNE BACON and EGGS, with PAN FRIED POTATOES	90

English Method of Preparation

To make certain that the Prime Ribs of Beef are tender and savory to the utmost, an old English method of preparation is followed. The main feature consists of coating the meat with a one-inch layer of rock salt. The heat, passing through the rock salt crystals, is distributed evenly and thoroughly. When the roast is ready, it presents a spectacular picture — with the facets of the crystals of rock salt flashing beautiful amber and brown tones. The shell of rock salt peels off in large sections, and the surprising thing is that no salt flavor is imparted to the roast or its natural juices. Our roasts are permitted to rest between one and two hours after coming out of the ovens, to be at their best when served; and the schedule of roasting is timed to complete the roasts one after the other to conform to the demand in the dining room. Our Chef will be pleased to show you the great roasts with their rock salt jackets in various steps of preparation.

Soups

SOUP du JOUR	15			BEEF CONSOMME	15
ONION SOUP au GRATIN	35	CREAM of TOMATO	25	JELLIED BEEF CONSOMME	15

★

Salad Bowl, a la Lawry

A delectable combination of crisp, fresh greens, thoroughly chilled.
With a full-flavored French dressing.
SERVED with ENTREES LISTED BELOW

Our Piece de Resistance
FROM THE ROAST CART
Roast Prime Ribs of Beef, au Jus
Yorkshire Pudding . . . Potatoes
Thick cut . . . **1.25**
"Diamond Jim" Brady's cut . . 1.75
(GOOD WINE ADDS TO THE ENJOYMENT OF FOOD . . . SEE WINE LIST ON REVERSE SIDE)

Braised SHORT PRIME RIBS of BEEF, a la Bourgeois (with Potatoes and fresh glazed Vegetables) en casserole	75
BROILED extra-thick PRIME RIB STEAK, Maitre d'Hotel, Julienne Potatoes	1.25
(COLD) Extra-thick ROAST PRIME RIBS OF BEEF	90
Broiled extra-thick LAMB CHOPS, glazed Pineapple, Julienne Potatoes	90

Browned and served in a skillet
ROAST PRIME RIBS of BEEF HASH, a la Lawry . . 65
With fried or poached egg . . 75
Southern Style . . 65

SALAD BOWL, a la Lawry . . . served with all ENTREES LISTED ABOVE

★

(HOT) ROAST PRIME RIBS of Beef SANDWICH, a la Lawry, on toasted French Bread; Whipped Potatoes . . . 85
(COLD) PRIME RIBS OF BEEF SANDWICH ON RUSSIAN RYE BREAD . . . 50

Vegetables

Fresh String Beans	20	Fresh Asparagus	25	
Fresh Green Peas	20	French-fried Onions	25	
		Fresh Lima Beans	20	

Potatoes

Julienne	15	Cottage Fried	20
French Fried	15	Au Gratin	25
		Baked	20

We reserve the right to refuse service to anyone. Not responsible for lost articles.

Sandwiches

Sliced BREAST OF CHICKEN	
LAWRY'S CLUB-HOUSE	
IMPORTED PRAGUE HAM, on Rye Bread	

Desserts

TOPS OFF A PERFECT REP...
Quarter of Fresh PINE...
served Hawaiian st...
35

Green Apple Pie	15	Fruit Jell...	
With American Cheese	25	Caramel...	
Ice Cream or Sherbet	15		

Cheese

Imported Swiss	25	Imported...	
Stilton	45	Imported...	
Gorgonzola with brandy	35	Cheddar w... Wine...	
New York American			

Coffee, Tea, Milk

Coffee	10	Tea (Pot)	
Demi-tasse	10	Certified Cu...	
Ice Coffee or Tea	15	Buttermilk	

★

Coffee Scientifically Brew...

According to latest scientific tests, practic... natural oils of coffee evaporate within thir... after grinding. By grinding our coffee an... it immediately, these natural oils are retain... ing a beverage that has a full-bodied arom... unusually rich, mellow flavor. Triple-filte... helps to achieve the finest in coffee goodne... coffee, of course, presupposes that the blend... carefully selected, and in this respect no... been spared.

Advertisement for Simpson's In The Strand, London, circa 1900s;
Lawry's The Prime Rib menu, 1938 COURTESY OF LAWRY'S

"CHURCHILL'S"
BROADWAY AND FORTY-NINTH STREET
NEW YORK

DANCING CHURCHILL'S CABARET

30913

"CHURCHILL'S," BROADWAY AND FORTY-NINTH STREET NEW YORK.

Chapter 2

ORIGINS OF THE SUPPER CLUB

1880-1919

To examine the origins of supper clubs, a brief review of the history of dining out and how we refer to it is in order. It is commonly understood that the first restaurant was opened in 1765 by a Parisian chef named Boulanger, who served "restorative broths" at his *bouillons restaurants*. However, there already were various words used to describe a restaurant, some of which date back to the mid-fifteenth century. They include *eating house*, *victualling-house*, *cook's shop*, *treating-house*, and *chop-shop*. The word *supper* is even older and dates back to the mid-thirteenth century French *soper* and was used to describe the last meal of the day. *Club* originated in the year 1593 as a transitive verb that meant "to unite or combine for a common cause."

Churchill's, New York City, 1912

11

The noun *supper club* arrived in 1844 and is defined as a restaurant or nightclub serving supper (*nightclub* was coined twenty-seven years after *supper club*). At the time, Wisconsin was still a wild frontier; it didn't become a state until 1848. Nearly one hundred years passed before Wisconsin's first supper clubs opened their doors. Yet, in New York City, residents were introduced to the art of fine dining in the early 1800s.

WANTED, a Sharp LAD. Must understand Bar Work. Good character indispensable. — Apply Supper Club, 12, Percy-street, Tottenham-court-road.

Classified advertisement, London, 1890

While there has never been an exact consensus of what makes a supper club a supper club, there has always been one common element: people sharing a late meal with others. In the 1800s, private social clubs in London's West End attracted a variety of members: aristocrats, professionals, politicians, artists, and actors. John Timbs writes in his book from 1866, *Club Life of London*, "The Club in the general acceptation of the term, may be regarded as one of the earliest offshoots of man's habitual gregariousness and social inclination." It was the actors, musicians, and artists of London's theaters that introduced the supper club to the world. When a new law went into effect that mandated a closing time of 12:30 a.m. for London's pubs and restaurants, it became difficult for actors and theatergoers to go out for a relaxing drink and meal after a show, which usually ended around 11:00 p.m. The solution was to join one of the newly emerging members-only clubs, which were able to stay open all night. These supper clubs, as they became known, were described by one writer as, "...a great boon after the theatre on Saturday night when the hotels and restaurants close at too absurdly early hours to be any good." With names like The New Corinthian Supper Club, The Percy Supper Club, and The New Camden Club, members and their guests enjoyed drinking, dining, and dancing from late night until dawn. Despite being well within the law regarding private clubs, they were often mired in controversy and frequently subjected to prosecution. Occasional raids for license violations, gambling, and complaints about noise and fighting brought fines or, worse, attempts to shut them down altogether. However, most clubs persevered and grew even more popular over the years; this may be due to the ease of acquiring a membership. The admission policy at supper clubs was not as rigorous compared to the other, more exclusive private clubs in London. An application for membership and payment of a small fee was usually all that was needed.

In New York City, dining out for pleasure was unheard of until 1827, when the Swiss-born Delmonico brothers, Pietro and Giovanni, along with their nephew Lorenzo Delmonico, converted their small confectionery shop into Delmonico's Restaurant Français (the name was later shortened to Delmonico's). It was the very first of its kind in the United States, and their innovations had a profound effect on dining out for well over a century. Delmonico's overnight success inspired a multitude

Delmonico's second location, 56 Beaver Street (aka 2-6 Williams Street), New York City, 1890. It is also the current location of Delmonico's. COURTESY OF NEW YORK PUBLIC LIBRARY

of new restaurants in New York City; it is estimated there were "hundreds" by the late 1800s. Dinner menus at that time consisted almost entirely of meat and organ dishes prepared in a variety of ways: roasted, stewed, and boiled. Fish and seafood were limited to what was available locally, including lobster, oysters, clams, cod, halibut, and American eel. Vegetable choices were similarly limited and consisted of potatoes, corn, spinach, peas, and onions. A common item on many menus was a relish course, which was often served at the beginning of the meal and consisted of pickled vegetables (more on this subject in Chapter 14). Supper, on the other hand, was a lighter meal served later in the evening, with smaller portion sizes. Choices for both supper and dinner were *à la carte*, one of the innovations introduced by Delmonico's. Some

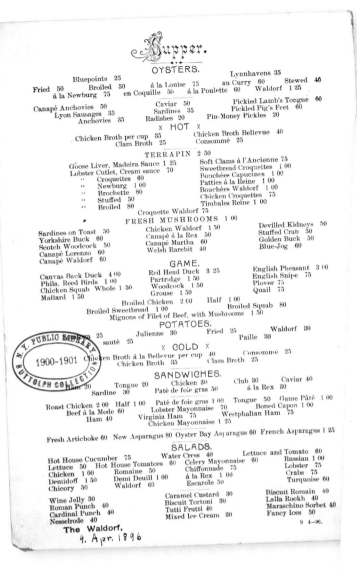

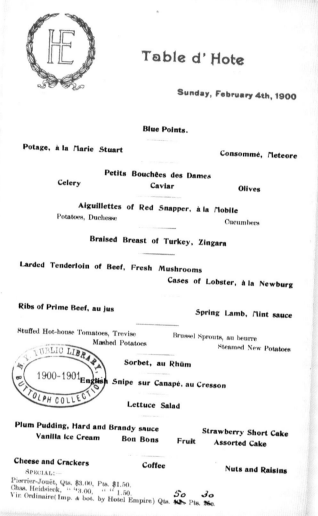

À la carte menu, The Waldorf, April 1896;
and Table d'Hote Hotel Empire 1900

restaurants still offered *table d'hôte*, a fixed menu for a set price (now often referred to as *prix fixe*). However, most customers enjoyed the freedom to select their own combination of dishes.

Word of London's "bohemian" supper clubs arrived in New York City in the late 1800s and began to influence the city's nightlife. In the days before radio, movies, and television, theaters provided nightly entertainment: highbrow operas, orchestras, and plays, as well as vaudeville and burlesque acts. Just as in London, New York's theater-goers sought establishments to enjoy some food and drinks after the shows let out. Lower-class patrons frequented taverns and saloons. For the well-heeled, expensive late-night suppers at hotels and restaurants and, in some cases, private clubs were their destination. In the summer of 1892, The New Vaudeville Club was founded; almost overnight, the private club attracted more than 2,500 members, which included many of the city's aristocratic families and businessmen. Among them were famed American architect Stanford White and industrialist William K. Vanderbilt I. Based on the Lyric Club in London, The New Vaudeville Club's mission was to provide a post-theatre variety show with supper and refreshments for its members and their wives between 11:00 p.m. and 1:00 a.m. in Madison Square Garden. A review from the *New York Sun* in January 1893 found the extravaganza unimpressive and noted that most members failed to attend further performances after a sold-out grand opening the night before. The *New York Times*, in a lengthy editorial, railed against the club and its entertainment: "It has no good reason for being. It is not likely to exert a beneficent influence upon either its members or the public." Ultimately, The New Vaudeville went bankrupt due to a lack of interest, and some of the remaining members turned their attention elsewhere.

At the time, New York's Tenderloin district, which ran from 24th to 42nd Streets, and between 5th and 7th Avenues, was home to most of the city's saloons, bordellos, gambling dens, dance halls, and several all-night restaurants. Located near the intersection of Broadway and 6th Avenue, these "supper restaurants" served meals during the day and early evening but came to life once theatre patrons began to arrive, around 11:00 p.m. They often stayed until dawn. According to the *New-York Tribune*, "These restaurants have resembled a supper club more than anything else. The same faces are to be seen in the same restaurants night after night. The best of order was usually maintained, but popping bottles and jest were the order of the night."

In April of 1895, a former waiter from the Waldorf Hotel named Frank Endres (also spelled in other sources as Endre and Endrus) formed The Supper Club on the upper floor of a café he leased at 150 West 34th Street. Based on "that well-known bohemian institution of London," the private membership consisted of the younger relatives of some of the best-known and wealthiest families in Manhattan (the president of The Supper Club was Frank De Peyster Hall, a wine merchant who lived at 635 Park Avenue). Male members and their female guests entered the club around midnight by way of the ladies' entrance to eat, drink, sing, and dance until the wee hours of the morning. The noisy revelers eventually caused a next-door neighbor, Dr. Allan Fitch, to complain to Endres. When that didn't work, Fitch went to the police. Captain Pickett and officers of the West 30th Street squad subsequently raided The Supper Club and found "several women and many men all in various stages of intoxication," as well as empty champagne bottles strewn around the floor. Despite this, the club continued to meet until Endres was arrested and his license was revoked by the Board of Excise. Undeterred, several months later, he reopened in a former hotel at 117 West 32nd Street under the name The Olympia Club. Once again, it became known for its wild parties, fights, and occasional improvised musical performances. However, it too was short-lived; in June of 1896, Endres defaulted on $1,123 owed to the New York Brewery Company for a loan to start the club and the lager beer served there. The sheriff ordered the club to close. The Olympia's closure was somberly noted with, ". . . the Tenderloin [lost] one of the very few abodes of Tenderloinness still remaining in it." Given the circumstances, Endres' club on West 34th Street may have been the first supper club in the US. It certainly was a novelty for New York City, considering the attention it received at the time. While there were other social clubs, like The New Vaudeville, they were nothing like the type Endres was operating. To begin with, The Supper Club members were much younger, and their all-night parties had more in common with the free-spirited London supper clubs. In addition, the goal of the other private clubs, including the New Vaudeville, was to provide entertainment and relaxation after a theatrical performance. The Supper Club's focus was a kind of rebellion against the rules and conventions of society. It was their own brand of hedonism—eat, drink, dance, sing, fight, and make whoopee. They were just ahead of their time.

1896 was also a bad year for other all-night restaurants. In March, the Raines law, named for Senator John W. Raines, went into effect. Among other restrictions, it set the closing time for bars at 1:00 a.m. While all-night restaurants were able to stay open beyond that hour, they had to stop serving drinks. Owners were faced with empty tables during what was otherwise their busiest time. The *New-York Tribune* observed, "The proprietors of the various places loudly bewail the ruining of their business, and the patron is equally bitter in the denunciation of a law that robs him of his drink with his nightly feast." One solution would have been to open private supper clubs similar to those in London, but that did not happen, possibly due to the reaction to the closing of The Supper Club and The Olympia Club. An 1898 article in the *New York Sun* noted, with an obvious reference to Frank Endres, "The supper club idea hangs about New York's social life like a phantom. That which appeals only to the men and includes dancing and drinking had a brief career which ended two years ago in bankruptcy and oblivion."

By the turn of the century, the unfavorable "bohemian" image of supper clubs had diminished somewhat, and they were viewed as slightly more respectable establishments. This shift began with a musical farce called *The Supper Club*, which opened on Christmas Eve, 1901, at the Winter Garden atop the New York Theatre in Long Acre Square (as Times Square was known then). *The Supper Club* had no plot; it resembled a vaudeville show with forty actors and singers, some of whom were well-known. The comedy routines included impersonations of prominent local politicians and law enforcement figures. The second of three acts was set in a fictional supper club in the Tenderloin and

COURTESY OF NEW YORK PUBLIC LIBRARY

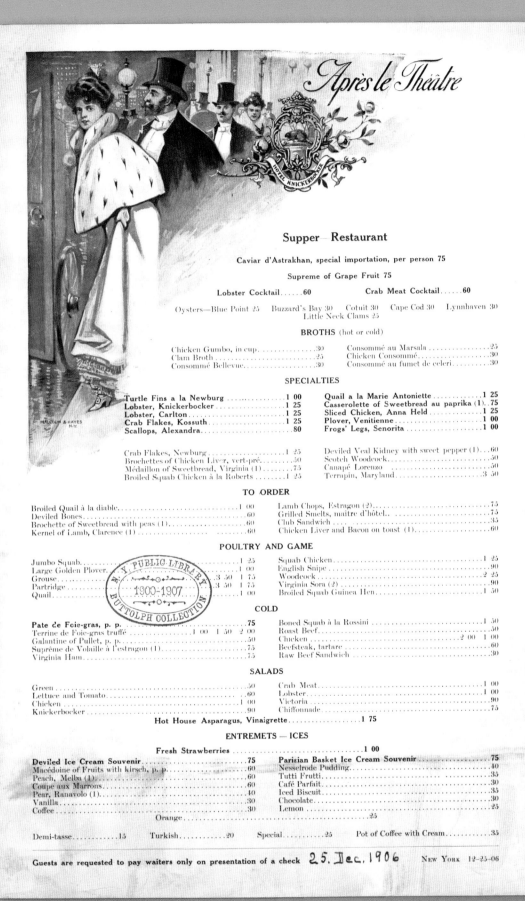

Après le Théâtre

Supper - Restaurant

Caviar d'Astrakhan, special importation, per person 75

Supreme of Grape Fruit 75

Lobster Cocktail......60   Crab Meat Cocktail......60

Oysters—Blue Point 25   Buzzard's Bay 30   Cotuit 30   Cape Cod 30   Lynnhaven 30
Little Neck Clams 25

BROTHS (hot or cold)

Chicken Gumbo, in cup......30	Consommé au Marsala......25
Clam Broth......25	Chicken Consommé......30
Consommé Bellevue......30	Consommé au fumet de celeri......30

SPECIALTIES

Turtle Fins a la Newburg......1 00	Quail a la Marie Antoniette......1 25
Lobster, Knickerbocker......1 25	Casserolette of Sweetbread au paprika (1)..75
Lobster, Carlton......1 25	Sliced Chicken, Anna Held......1 25
Crab Flakes, Kossuth......1 25	Plover, Venitienne......1 00
Scallops, Alexandra......80	Frogs' Legs, Senorita......1 00
Crab Flakes, Newburg......1 25	Deviled Veal Kidney with sweet pepper (1)...60
Brochettes of Chicken Liver, vert-pré......50	Scotch Woodcock......50
Médaillon of Sweetbread, Virginia (1)......75	Canapé Lorenzo......50
Broiled Squab Chicken à la Roberts......1 25	Terrapin, Maryland......3 50

TO ORDER

Broiled Quail à la diable......1 00	Lamb Chops, Estragon (2)......75
Deviled Bones......60	Grilled Smelts, maitre d'hôtel......75
Brochette of Sweetbread with peas (1)......60	Club Sandwich......35
Kernel of Lamb, Clarence (1)......60	Chicken Liver and Bacon on toast (1)......60

POULTRY AND GAME

Jumbo Squab......1 25	Squab Chicken......1 25
Large Golden Plover......1 00	English Snipe......90
Grouse......3 50 1 75	Woodcock......2 25
Partridge......3 50 1 75	Virginia Sora (2)......90
Quail......1 00	Broiled Squab Guinea Hen......1 50

COLD

Pate de Foie-gras, p. p.......75	Boned Squab à la Rossini......1 50
Terrine de Foie-gras truffé......1 00 1 50 2 00	Roast Beef......50
Galantine of Pullet, p. p.......50	Chicken......2 00 1 00
Suprême de Volaille à l'estragon (1)......75	Beefsteak, tartare......60
Virginia Ham......75	Raw Beef Sandwich......30

SALADS

Green......50	Crab Meat......1 00
Lettuce and Tomato......60	Lobster......1 00
Chicken......1 00	Victoria......90
Knickerbocker......90	Chiffonnade......75

Hot House Asparagus, Vinaigrette......1 75

ENTREMETS — ICES

Fresh Strawberries......1 00

Deviled Ice Cream Souvenir......75	Parisian Basket Ice Cream Souvenir......75
Macédoine of Fruits with kirsch, p. p.......60	Nesselrode Pudding......40
Peach, Melba (1)......60	Tutti Frutti......35
Coupe aux Marrons......60	Café Parfait......30
Pear, Ranavolo (1)......40	Iced Biscuit......35
Vanilla......30	Chocolate......30
Coffee......30	Lemon......25

Orange......25

Demi-tasse......15   Turkish......20   Special......25   Pot of Coffee with Cream......35

Guests are requested to pay waiters only on presentation of a check   25. Dec. 1906   NEW YORK   12-25-06

featured a series of women singing while dressed in "cheap, but gay" gowns. Throughout the show, the audience cheered at the mention of local wines and whiskeys, meant as advertisements. However, in a scathing, front-page review of its opening, a theatre critic for the *New York Times* claimed a night spent with a dead body in a morgue was a more favorable use of time. The review continued, "Of all the punk ever put on a stage *The Supper Club* has a large slice off the top." The *New-York Tribune* offered a more middling take: "Whatever may have been thought of the quality of the entertainment, nobody could complain that there was not enough of it." Despite playwright Sydney Rosenfeld's decision to title the production *The Supper Club*, there remained the question of how to define the term. In reviewing another Broadway play that contained a scene set in a London supper club, one writer expressed frustration: "We do not know much about supper clubs now or how they differ from suppers without clubs or clubs without suppers. Some of us may object peevishly to late suppers, but not on strictly moral grounds."

In 1903, the very genteel Brook Club was established. The *New York Times* curiously referred to it as, "Really the first supper club in New York." The writer continued, "There are numerous institutions of this kind in London, where it is almost impossible to get anything to eat after midnight. It is getting to be the same way in New York and clubs like the Brook will be established, especially in the theatre districts." Its male-only membership consisted of New York's high society; Stanford White was a

LOUIS MARTIN'S, BROADWAY AND 42ND ST., N. Y.   A VIEW OF MAIN FLOOR

Postcard, Louis Martin's, 1911

member, as well as horse-breeder William K. Vanderbilt II, among others. The Brook Club, named after Alfred Lord Tennyson's 1886 poem, "The Brook," offered late-night meals in a "homelike" atmosphere and also offered private bedrooms to which guests could retire when they tired of reveling. One year later, the *Times* pronounced the private club a success: "The Brook is not alone an all-night or a supper club; it has just as large a gathering in the afternoons as at night."

In April of 1904, in anticipation of the *New York Times* moving their new headquarters to the Times Tower on Broadway and 7th Avenue, Mayor George B. McClellan signed a resolution to rename Long Acre Square to Times Square. In subsequent years, further development of the Times Square area included even more grand theaters and new, massive restaurants like Churchill's, Rector's, and Louis Martin's. These dining palaces were as big as department stores and staffed by hundreds, which enabled them to seat as many as 600 customers at one time. Louis Martin's, at 42nd and Broadway, claimed to be the largest restaurant in the world, with room for 2,400 diners spread out over seven stories and staffed by nearly 500 employees working out of four kitchens. The ornate exteriors of these dining halls were matched by intricately adorned interiors, many of which bore the lush, palm garden style that was popular at the time. They offered lunch, dinner, late-night supper, and dancing and were nicknamed "trotteries" due to the trendy ragtime-era dance, the Turkey Trot.

Postcard, Yates Restaurant, 1912

The after-theater crowd in the Times Square area numbered in the thousands due to the large number of theaters. In addition to dancing, some restaurants offered cabaret shows for the late-night diners. Cabaret mania spread so quickly it was dubbed "Cabarazy" by one journalist. Not everyone was on board with this, however; some restaurants made a point to advertise they did not offer cabaret or dancing and were just a quiet, more respectable alternative for dining. Victorian attitudes led to complaints about cabaret licensing and what some considered lurid adult entertainment, which quickly drew the attention of City Hall. In 1912, restauranteur Louis Martin and his cabaret manager were arrested after detectives observed alcohol being served while a dance called the "Wiggle Wiggle" (described as "more suggestive than the Turkey Trot") was performed. A judge later ruled in Martin's favor, which opened the door for more cabaret shows at restaurants, at least for the time being.

It was in this atmosphere in the early 1900s when newspaper headlines and word of mouth rebranded supper clubs as social events and society affairs, seemingly overnight. Initially referred to as *club suppers*, the words switched places and became the new standard. Supper club announcements soon filled the society pages in both metropolitan and small-town newspapers across the country. These group supper clubs met weekly or monthly and adopted names, like the Six O'Clock Club, The Twilight Club, Young Married People Supper Club, or simply the Y.W.C.A. Supper Club. They gathered for an evening meal and a presentation on a timely topic from a noted guest speaker. While private clubs and the early supper clubs were strictly for male members—women were considered guests—it was now married women who hosted friends or groups of married couples at their homes for supper and card games.

"If We Were Alone," She Whispered, "I Should Want You to Kiss Me!"

Supper Club illustration from *The Hillman, An Unusual Love Story*, 1917

They also arranged post-theatre supper club dances held at hotel ballrooms. These were more formal affairs; men dressed in black tie and tails, and women wore their finest gowns. Around this time, women also followed E. Phillips Oppenheim's *The Hillman, An Unusual Love Story*, a syndicated serial published in newspapers across the country. Set in present-day England, it concerned the adventures of actress Louise Maurel and her friend and fellow actress, Sophy. One particular installment published in the *Marshfield News and Wisconsin Hub* on September 13, 1917, occurs in a London supper club called the Aldwych. While fictional, the story offers a fairly accurate, if overly sentimental, description of what one was like at the time:

The cab stopped a few minutes later outside what seemed to be a private house. The door was opened at once. Sophy wrote John's name in the book and they were ushered by the manager, who had come forward to greet them, into a long room, brilliantly lit, and filled, except in the center, with supper tables. John looked around him wonderingly. The popping of champagne corks was almost incessant. A slightly voluptuous atmosphere of cigarette smoke, mingled with the perfumes shaken from the clothes and hair of the women, several more of whom were now dancing, hung about the place.

"Isn't this rather nice?" she whispered. "Do you like being here with me, Mr. John Strangewey?"

"Of course I do," he answered heartily. "Is this a restaurant?"

She shook her head.

"No, it's a club. We can sit here all night, if you like."

"Can I join?" he asked.

She laughed as she sent for a form and made him fill it in.

"Tell me," he begged, as he looked around him, "who are these girls? They look so pretty and well-dressed, and yet so amazingly young to be out at this time of night."

"Mostly actresses," she replied, "and musical comedy girls. I was in musical-comedy myself before Louise rescued me."

Later, John tells Louise about his night out with Sophy:

"We went to a supper club last night and stayed there till about half past three."

"Really," said Louise, "I am not sure that I approve of this! A supper club with Sophy until half past three in the morning!"

Meanwhile, the cabarets in New York City and other big cities around the country became a prominent feature of city nightlife in hotels, cafés, and restaurants. Cabarets existed on two tiers: the high-class and respectable dances usually found in hotels and the more unrestrained merrymaking accompanied by jazz played in dance halls, night resorts, and supper restaurants. This newly emerging jazz consisted of a mixture of ragtime, blues, and patriotic marches and was becoming all the rage. Female singers dressed in tights specialized in risqué songs and alluring gyrations (like that Wiggle Wiggle), and they often sang while mingling in the audience, focusing their attention on the men. To some, cabaret bred immorality and depravity; they felt the practice of singing and dancing where liquor was served should be abolished.

Still, regulating such a popular form of entertainment wasn't easy, despite the support of prominent citizens and church groups. Milwaukee's Chief of Police John T. Janssen clashed with Mayor Gerhard A. Bading over a proposed anti-cabaret ordinance in the fall of 1915. Despite Bading's veto, the ordinance was passed by the common council, who supported Janssen. A year later, a similar ordinance in Racine was opposed by hotel owner John Wagner, who said, "They have cut out the cabaret in Milwaukee, and anyone will tell you who has been there, that Milwaukee is the deadest town in the United States." Racine's mayor T.W. Thiesen referred to the cabaret as "garbage" and added, "The women walk around the tables and make fools of the men and even of the women. I object to those things. The women are loud in their ways. It is not the object of this council to eliminate decently run places." Kenosha's police chief Owen O'Hare also called for a ban on cabaret. He said, "I have been watching this thing for some time and I have found that the women singing in the saloon have a demoralizing effect."

Chicago, where there were an estimated 2,000 cabarets and even more saloons, spent years fighting to control them; however, they continued to prosper. Daily articles in Chicago newspapers detailed the more notorious cabarets where prostitution, underage drinking, and other crimes were taking place. In May of 1918, the city passed a new ordinance that banned liquor from establishments that hosted cabaret and dancing. Curiously, the law passed with the support of the Chicago Brewers' Association (CBA), who aligned themselves with church organizations and reformers. The CBA argued that the cabaret was a detriment to the decent saloon, and as a result, helped turn public sentiment toward shutting down all drinking establishments. William Legner, president of the CBA, said, "Now is the time for the renaissance of the saloon. Chicago should . . . take the initial step toward putting the saloon on a better, cleaner basis that will bring it popular approval." Edward R. Diedrich, an attorney for the CBA, was more direct: "The average cabaret today is a recruiting place for evil. We must pull out the cabaret business by its roots."

To the east, in New York City, it was a waiters' strike, and not the influenza epidemic, that temporarily closed some of Manhattan's biggest restaurants and hotel dining rooms in 1918. One year earlier, some of those same restaurants in the "cabaret belt," including Churchill's, Healy's, and Rector's, were surprised by a 10 percent "war tax" on food, drinks, and table reservations. In addition, restaurants across the country reduced the amount of food they served in compliance with a mandate from the US Food Administration, then led by Herbert Hoover, to help supply the military and Allies. Overnight, menus changed from *à la carte* to *table d'hôte* to minimize food waste. Portions of meat, fish, and fowl could not weigh more than seven ounces; cheese was limited to one-half ounce per person, and bread and rolls were limited to two ounces. Bacon could not be served as a garnish, which meant club sandwiches were absolutely taboo.

Hoover also ordered a 30 percent reduction in the amount of grain available to the brewing industry, and legal beer was limited to 2.75 percent alcohol by weight. As a result, many cabarets in big cities across the country that depended on the profit from the sale of liquor struggled to stay open. Some got by with "punchless punch," selling grape juice, ginger ale, lemonade, and buttermilk at high prices. Entertainment was eliminated in some establishments to save money. The cutbacks were intended to be temporary; however, the Eighteenth Amendment was making its way through the state legislatures and was ratified on January 16, 1919.

PROHIBITION AND THE VOLSTEAD ACT

The contentious debate about whether to ban the manufacture and sale of alcohol in the United States had been going on for much of the 1800s. It wasn't until Congress passed the Eighteenth Amendment on December 18, 1917, that Prohibition became law—if the states ratified the measure within seven years. On November 18, 1918, just seven days after the armistice that ended World War I was signed, Congress passed the Wartime Prohibition Act. It was a temporary measure to save grain for the war effort by restricting the sale of beverages containing more than 2.75 percent alcohol. The Act took effect on June 30, 1919. Tens of thousands of brewery workers were laid off, but they expected to be rehired when the Act ended.

However, on January 16, 1919, thirty-six of the forty-eight states (Hawaii and Alaska did not enter the Union until 1959) ratified the Eighteenth Amendment. This sparked a debate between the "drys" (the Republican majority) and the "wets" (mostly Democrats) in Congress over whether to permanently ban the manufacture and sale of alcohol or repeal the wartime prohibition. Minnesota Republican Congressman Andrew Volstead, who was the chairman of the House Judiciary Committee, introduced new legislation that defined the processes and procedures for banning alcoholic beverages, as well as their production and distribution. The Volstead Act, as it was known, put the teeth in the enforcement of the Eighteenth Amendment. "The American people have said that they do not want any liquor sold, and they have said it emphatically by passing almost unanimously the constitutional amendment," Chairman Volstead argued. The Republican majority agreed, and the law, which was initially vetoed by President Woodrow Wilson, was passed on October 28, 1919. The "Noble Experiment," as Herbert Hoover called it, began on January 17, 1920. It lasted nearly thirteen years, ending after Wisconsin Republican Senator John W. Blaine introduced legislation that led to the passage of the Twenty-First Amendment and the repeal of Prohibition on December 5, 1933.

Beer, Song And Dance Tabooed For Cabarets

MILWAUKEE, Wis.— Cabaret dancing is prohibited even as an accompaniment to one-half per cent near beer, according to an opinion furnished Mayor Daniel W. Hoan today by the city attorneys' office.

The opinion says in part:

"The cabaret ordinance prohibits dancing, singing, or any entertainment of whatsoever nature commonly classed under the term 'cabaret' in all places licensed to sell strong, spirituous, malt, ardent or intoxicating liquors."

The HIGH and DIZZY
COMEDY Thriller!
HARRY LANGDON
"SLIM" SUMMERVILLE
BESSIE LOVE
CARL LAEMMLE
Presents
SEE AMERICA
THIRST
UNIVERSAL Picture

Chapter 3

NEW YORK CITY SPEAKEASIES AND CABARET

1920-1934

"The knell of the cabaret was sounded when the specter of Total Abstinence stalked through the front door! No cabaret can be sustained on ginger ale and near-beer." Or so one New York writer predicted as the "noble experiment" of Prohibition began. Owners of the restaurants and cafés of Broadway surprised everyone by reversing course; they invested in brighter and more spectacular productions on the theory that cheap costumes and scenery don't as easily fool sober customers.

See America Thirst,
Universal Pictures,
1930

At Churchill's, cabaret began at dinner, went all night, and featured dancing by The Norrie Sisters, Thelma Carleton, and the Rackos. Café de Paris (formally known as Rector's) had been converted into a high-class grill and rotisserie with a newly renovated ballroom for dancing. Thomas Healy's Golden Glades continued its popular ice ballets, along with a comedy revue ironically titled, "Cheer Up New York." At the Café des Beaux-Arts, which was often described as "Paris in New York," owner Andre Bustanoby offered nightly Beaux-Arts Supper Club dances, under the supervision of Miss Kathryn McCarthy and Miss Jet Hahlo. According to the *New York Herald*, the result of these changes meant that "every restaurant in the theatrical district [has] record-breaking crowds each night and record prices are being paid without a grumble."

But the reality was that many people still wanted to enjoy a drink. It wasn't long before speakeasies started popping up like weeds all over the five boroughs of New York. Not all of them were makeshift joints hidden behind a false storefront; some were new, out in the open—part cabaret and part speakeasy. O. O. McIntyre, known as "The Man Who Taught America About New York" by way of his syndicated column, *New York Day By Day*, wrote about this phenomenon on February 9, 1922:

It is 2:00 a.m. The hour of the sensuous soiree in the midnight supper clubs. The inconspicuous entrances are encircled with chinchilla wraps and silk hats, whose wearers are trying to pass the silken ropes. For in the hard atmosphere of the tiny supper clubs, which have killed the cabaret, the dances are weekly growing more sensual and popular. They are called 'clubs' but no admission is charged. The smaller they are the more they appeal. One seats fifty and it is necessary to make reservations weeks in advance. The ceilings are hung low with a silken canopy and the walls draped with satin in which lights are half hidden. And the performers—most of them young and beautiful and a little bit abashed. It is a phase of nightlife that New York has never seen before. The patrons are not bummers or slummers, but people whose wealth and social position are historic. Women in $1000 gowns and pearls and diamonds to grace a Sheba. Men who have progressed triumphantly in business and the arts. They sit at tiny tables openly drinking heady wines, all smoking and flushed with a new thrill. A modern age amusement mad!

O. O. McIntyre, 1928

McIntyre's commentary and others like it were instrumental in creating interest in this "new thrill." Women were exploring the freedom that was an unforeseen consequence of Prohibition. Going out all night, drinking, smoking, dancing—who needs those old-fashioned dinner parties at home? The scandalous headlines describing

Golden Pheasant Supper Club

not all of these new supper clubs were exclusive to New York City. One was located 400 miles northwest of midtown Manhattan, in the little hamlet of Greenhurst, New York. The Golden Pheasant Supper Club was situated on the southeastern shoreline of Chatauqua Lake, just north of Jamestown (the birthplace of Lucille Ball). The supper club was opened in 1925 by H. Laverne Lindstrom and featured live entertainment, dining, and dancing until 4:00 a.m. or later, six nights per week. The menu was a curious mix of Chinese and German dishes along with steak, chicken, and fish. High-priced soft drinks, including "lime and lithia," a precursor to 7UP, White Rock mineral water, and ginger ale were sold as set-ups, or mixers, for liquor supplied by the customer.

Chatauqua Lake was a popular tourist destination and was served by the New York Central and Pennsylvania rail lines, which connected New York, Pittsburgh, Cleveland, and other major cities. This enabled the Golden Pheasant to offer a variety of regional and national entertainers, including Jimmy Durante's Big Dinner Club Revue, Mildred Harris, "Queen of the Nite Club Whoopee," and Ed Houston's New Yorkster's, "Direct from Harlem."

Despite being advertised as "Chatauqua Lake's Fun Spot," the club fell into hard times after Prohibition as competition from newly opened clubs drew customers away. In 1934, it was the unfortunate site of a murder-suicide. A few years later, in November 1937, a fire destroyed the building. H. Laverne Lindstrom died only two months later in a hospital in San Antonio, Texas.

supper clubs only added to their notoriety and appeal. The news of a 1922 breach of promise trial between Gilliard T. Boag, a well-known Broadway cabaret entrepreneur, and his mistress, Miss Petronella Cline, detailed the fortune he was making from the sale of liquor at several of his supper clubs, including the Piccadilly Rendezvous and the Little Club, both located at 121 West 45th Street, and Club Royal, at 9 East 52nd Street. Miss Cline testified that the clubs opened at midnight and furnished refreshment, entertainment, and dancing. Two years later, a federal judge padlocked Boag's Piccadilly Rendezvous under the Volstead Act's nuisance clause, along with the Silver Slipper, which two vaudeville actors owned.

By the mid-1920s, liquor flowed freely at dozens of supper clubs around New York, although it was poured at a premium. A night out put a serious dent in one's wallet if it didn't empty it altogether. Cover charges ranged from 50¢ to $3 per person ($7 to $43 in 2020); exclusive clubs charged $5 ($73) and up. Scotch whiskey sold for $5 to $10 a pint ($73 to $146) and champagne was an eye-watering $12 to $25 a quart ($175 to $365). Even bottled water was a hefty $2 ($29), and club sandwiches were $1.50 ($21). The high prices were necessary to compensate entertainers, who made anywhere from $700 to $2,500 per week ($10,243 to $36,583). Many performing artists began their illustrious careers in supper clubs, including the dancing teams of Fred Astaire and his sister Adele, Clifton Webb and his partner Mary Hay, comedian Jimmy Durante, and singer Sophie Tucker, who eventually operated her own club. Chorus girls averaged $50 to $150 per week ($731 to $2,195). Hostesses were available to dance with single men and were paid little, but they usually made a small fortune in tips. House bands were paid $800 to $4,000 a week ($11,706 to $58,533), and head waiters took in as much as $2,500 a month ($36,583). Weekly expenses also included payments to local officials to look the other way. To many, the spirited gaiety of a night out was well worth the actual cost. With the stock market booming and bathtub gin flowing, the Roaring Twenties were in full effect. Decadence had never felt so good—and few cared about the risks.

Even though corruption kept the clubs open, not everyone was able to be bought. On October 20, 1925, under the headline "Gotham Cabaret Clean Up Opens—Thirty Broadway Supper Houses Hit by Prohibition Drive," newspapers across the country detailed the summonses and complaints that were served to supper club owners by Emory Buckner, the US district attorney for the Southern District of New York. He planned to padlock over one hundred Manhattan night resorts, starting with the El Fey, Lido Venice, Piping Rock, Game Cock, Piccadilly Supper Club, Half Moon, Hotsy Totsie, and others. Some had been padlocked before and were again, including the El Fey, whose owner Larry Fay was called the "originator of the night, or supper club idea" by the *Daily News*.

Following the release of *The Jazz Singer*, the first full-length film with synchronized sound, in 1927, Hollywood experienced a transformation. The "talkies" portrayed a risqué combination of booze, sex, and violence that was only tamed by the studios' eventual self-censorship, dictated by the Production Code Administration (PCA) in late 1934. Films made prior to this were later known as the pre-Code era

Sheboygan Theatre, 1932;
Parkway Theatre, Madison, 1928

of Hollywood. Pre-Code films often featured New York City speakeasies, night-clubs, and dance halls, which provided audiences with an eye-opening glimpse into a world they likely only knew from newspaper headlines. In the 1928 Warner Bros. feature *Lights of New York*, two unwitting barbers are duped into allowing their barbershop to become a front for a speakeasy called The Night Hawk. RKO's 1930 release *Framed* features supper club hostess Evelyn Brent, who welcomes customers with, "If you don't see what you want, ask for it, we've got it alright! Yes sir, right off the boat—our motto is 'Make hay while the sun shines and make whoopee with the moonshine!'" Universal's 1932 film *Night World* shows scantily-clad chorus girls cavorting at Happy's Club. Boris Karloff plays Happy, a mild-mannered club owner who is bumped off by mobsters while Lew Ayres battles the bottle and gets the girl. By 1930, 100 million movie tickets were sold per week. Depression-era Hollywood provided the movie-hungry public with an escape to places they might never see in person. "We took the position that motion pictures should depict and reflect American life," said director Clarence Brown, "and cocktail parties and speakeasies were definitely a part of that life."

Chapter 4

WISCONSIN'S FIRST SUPPER CLUBS

1920-1934

"When I sell liquor, it's called bootlegging; when my patrons serve it on Lake Shore Drive, it's called hospitality." —AL CAPONE

Marge Gogian,
The Turk's Inn,
Hayward
COURTESY OF VARUN
KATARIA

As Prohibition began, some of that hospitality served to the city of Chicago was from Wisconsin. Because the state's breweries were permitted to produce nothing stronger than "near beer"—one-half of 1 percent alcohol—home brew and moonshine quickly found their way into speakeasies, roadhouses, dance halls, and soda parlors. If one wanted real whiskey, doctors, dentists, and even veterinarians were able to write legal prescriptions for a pint or more. People found ways to get it—and profit from it.

One enterprising milkman in Kenosha kept customers on his route happy with home deliveries of hooch until a teetotaler called the cops. From the start, Prohibition was unpopular with most Wisconsinites, and by 1926, voters had approved a referendum asking Congress to allow for the manufacture and sale of beer with 2.75 percent alcohol. In 1929, more than two-thirds of Wisconsin's "Wets" voted for the elimination of the state's enforcement of the Volstead Act, putting it solely in the hands of the federal government to implement. With the saloons all dried up, where could folks get a beer with their fish fry?

They served both at the roadhouse. Located outside city limits, roadhouses were inns and taverns that were open seven days a week and served simple, affordable food like hamburgers, sandwiches, fried chicken, and fish. During Prohibition, they earned an unsavory reputation as a place where booze, loose women, and gambling were found. During the 1920s and early '30s, there was perpetual discussion in newspapers about their depravity. An editorial in the *Sheboygan Press* in 1932 stated, "Roadhouses were the creation of prohibition and you will have them as long as you have prohibition, and any attempt to abolish them will prove futile. A public dance hall is a

A padlocked and condemned saloon papered with advertisements, Milwaukee, 1929

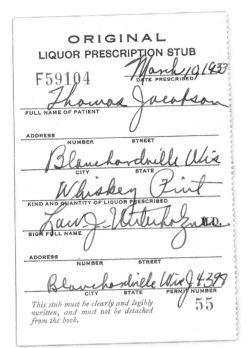

Whiskey prescription, 1933   Point's Special near-beer

roadhouse and you can't get around it. How are you going to distinguish between the two?" State Representative John E. Cashman was concerned, too: "[The] evil influence of the roadhouse and beer farm dance hall [is] usually established and patronized by the worst city elements."

Local authorities did their best to pass legislation to tame them or shutter them entirely, but nothing seemed to work. In 1925, the temporary closing of the Midway Inn on Bluemound Road in Milwaukee County was hailed as the "death knell" for roadhouses. The Inn's owner had been charged with allowing customers to consume their own alcohol by using set-ups—ginger ale and White Rock for $1.75, together with a spoon for use in picking up ice. Attorneys for the Midway Inn appealed the verdict, and the roadhouse reopened and was permitted to continue to operate. Despite these setbacks, authorities persisted. In 1928, twenty-four roadhouses in Kenosha County were padlocked under temporary federal injunctions by Circuit Judge E. B. Belden. Among the nine saloons downtown and fifteen roadhouses in the county were The White Swan and Travelers' Inn in Silver Lake, the Parkway Inn on South Sheridan Road, the Sheridan Road Inn on Highway 15, the Orchard Inn on Highway 50, Mozzerelli's Poolroom at 1918 57th Street, and Stanley's Place, The Tent, the Spanish Tavern, Paris Gardens, and Theleen's Place, all located on State Highway 41. Some had been padlocked before; one roadhouse owner, Paul Wojt, owner of The White Swan, received his third padlock in four years.

University of Wisconsin-Madison Professor Dean Goodnight issued a warning to students about roadhouses, describing them as an "up-to-the-minute den of iniquity" and the "more subtle and vicious successor of the old-time saloon." While his intentions were good, he was practically making a sales pitch for them: "The roadhouse is

SURVEY OF PROHIBITION ENFORCEMENT IN WISCONSIN

Conducted by Frank Buckley, Bureau of Prohibition, Treasury Department. His twenty-four-page report detailed several topics, including the population (2,953,000), legislation, enforcement, federal and state personnel, classification of arrests, and deaths from alcohol. One of the more entertaining lists detailed how much drinking was going on—dry, wet, or very wet—in all seventy-one counties and whether the sheriff was cooperative. In an opening statement to the report, Buckley wrote, "Wisconsin, to the average American unacquainted with actual conditions therein, is commonly regarded as a Gibraltar of the wets—sort of a Utopia where everybody drinks their fill and John Barleycorn still holds forth in splendor."

County, Sheriff, Conditions, 1929

Adams, No cooperation, Wet.
Ashland, ---, Wet.
Barron, Will cooperate, Wet.
Bayfield, No cooperation, Wet.
Brown, ---, Wet. Green Bay; prostitution, padlocked 69 soft drink saloons in 1928.
Buffalo, ---, Wet.
Burnett, Good, Dry.
Calumet, No cooperation, Wet. An alcohol county.
Chippewa, Good, Wet.
Clark, Will cooperate, ---
Columbia, Good, Good county attorney, Dry.
Crawford, No cooperation, Wet.
Dane, Will cooperate, Wet. Madison.
Dodge, ---, ---.
Door, No cooperation, Very Wet.
Douglas, ---, Wet. prostitution; good chief of police at Superior.
Dunn, No cooperation, Dry.
Eau Claire, Will cooperate, Wet.
Florence, No cooperation, Very sparsely settled; heavily wooded.
Fond du Lac, Good, Weak county attorney.
Forest, Cooperate, Sparsely settled; heavily wooded, settled by Kentuckians who distill.
Grant, Very good, Dry.
Green, Good, Wet. Swiss element.
Green Lake, No cooperation, Wet.
Iowa, ---, Dry.
Iron, Bad, Very Wet. Gambling, prostitution, general lawlessness in Hurley.
Jackson, Good, Dry. Active county attorney.
Jefferson, No cooperation, Wet.
Juneau, Will cooperate, Wet. County attorney murdered - ex-sheriff held for crime; both involved with liquor ring.
Kenosha, ---, Wet. County attorney elected by wets; large foreign element.
Kewaunee, No cooperation, Wet.
La Crosse, Will cooperate, Wet.
Lafayette, Good, Effective county attorney.
Langlade, No cooperation, Wet.
Lincoln, Will cooperate, Wet.
Manitowoc, ---, Wet. Wildest breweries.
Marathon, No cooperation, Very Wet.
Marinette, Good, Wet.
Marquette, Will cooperate, Number of town marshalls active in liquor work.

County, Sheriff, Conditions, 1929, cont'd.

Milwaukee, ---, , Wet. Splendid chief of police in Milwaukee; prostitution; 1,217 soft-drink parlors in telephone book all sell liquor.
Monroe, Good , Dry.
Oconto, No cooperation, Wet. Timber Country.
Oneida, ---, Wet.
Outagamie, ---, Wet. City of Appleton; source of alcohol for Wisconsin, Minnesota and Dakotas.
Ozaukee, Will cooperate, Wet.
Pepin, No cooperation, Moist.
Pierce, Will cooperate, Dry.
Polk, ---, ---.
Portage, No cooperation, Wet. Good county attorney.
Price, ---, Wet. Fair conditions.
Racine, ---, Wet. County attorney good.
Richland, Will cooperate, Dry.
Rock, Good cooperation, Dry.
Rusk, Will cooperate, Dry.
St. Croix, No cooperation, Dry.
Sauk, ---, Wet.
Sawyer, Will cooperate, Dry.
Shawano, Cooperates, Dry. Menomonee Indian reservation; good cooperation from Indian agent.
Sheboygan, Poor, Very Wet. Prostitution; gambling; sheriff and county attorney in recent controversy, blamed each other.
Taylor, No cooperation, Very Wet.
Trempleau, Will cooperate, Dry.
Vernon, Good cooperation, Dry.
Vilas, Will cooperate, Wet.
Walworth, ---, Fairly Dry. Good county attorney; large German element.
Washburn, ---, Dry.
Washington, ---, Wet.
Waukesha, ---, Both sheriff and county attorney wet, but will cooperate.
Waupaca, Cooperates, Dry. Home of Senator Severson, sponsor of late Wisconsin dry law.
Waushara, Good, Dry. Good county attorney.
Winnebago, No cooperation, Wet. Oshkosh and Menasha wet cities; wildest breweries; county attorney good - bad sheriff ousted for liquor dereliction.
Wood, Will cooperate, Wet.

DANCING
At The
CLAVA DEL RIO
Green Bay's Smartest
Night Club
Nothing Under—Nothing
Over 25c.
Cover 25c — Soda 25c

ANDY'S PLACE DANCE PAVILION AND TAVERN
BIRCHWOOD   WISCONSIN
44 -- 118

Nightclub advertisement, 1933; a rural roadhouse, dance hall, and filling station, circa 1940s

more subtle because it ... obeys the law and does not purvey liquor, but merely provides attractions for those who carry it and a rendezvous for bootleggers and customers."

In 1928, public drunkenness in Fond du Lac was a big problem, despite the lack of legal saloons. The city had 113 roadhouses, dance halls, and soda parlors licensed to sell non-intoxicating drinks. However, according to the Chief of Police James Silgen, only two of these establishments attempted to abide by the law; they ultimately failed. Silgen believed the soft drink parlor was a subterfuge for the saloon because it was the rendezvous for young people who wanted to get drunk. Deputy Sheriff Fred W. Schlaak of Fond du Lac County defended the roadhouses and soda parlors by saying, "The biggest contributing factor to crime and delinquency today is the rural dance hall. It is not the soft drink parlors or the roadhouses, but these dance halls that do the damage. The young people, boys and girls in the schools, go out to these dance halls. The bootleggers attend these dances 'in force' and well supplied with flasks filled with moonshine whisky. There is drinking outside the hall and in cars within a radius of several blocks. I have heard rumors of these bootleggers having as high as fifty flasks at a dance."

It might seem absurd to claim that a dance hall caused more trouble than a place called The Broken Knuckle, but dance halls did attract a younger, presumably more innocent crowd. Drinking was bad enough, and combined with boys and girls gyrating to deafening jazz music, and other such promiscuous behavior, dance halls were seen by many as immoral. This led to several ordinances regulating dance halls across the state. In 1923, a large crowd of spectators in Wausau cheered when Marathon County supervisors unanimously adopted more severe regulations on its local dance halls. In Kenosha County, their dance hall mandate went so far as to ban the Charleston from dance floors.

These restrictions may seem baffling, but remember, rural dance halls were a relatively new phenomenon in the 1920s. Besides attracting teens and young adults, they provided an opportunity to mingle with the opposite sex and experiment with smoking and drinking beyond the watchful eye of their parents. Some dance halls in Wisconsin were used by the community for other purposes, like weddings, banquets, and town meetings. Others were dedicated to holding dances regularly and were often part of a saloon. A hall accommodated anywhere from fifty to several hundred people or more. In Wisconsin, the minimum age to enter was sixteen, but children as young as thirteen were often found among the others. Refreshments were limited to soft drinks, but many in the crowd stashed bottles of alcohol in their pockets called *hippers*. Bootleggers showed up to sell whiskey out of their cars in the parking lot; the next day, the litter of empty bottles were scattered around nearby lots. Complaints about "the wail and blare of the saxophones and trombones" that went on until the early morning hours were common. Prostitution was also a serious matter, as men outnumbered women by a considerable margin; the admission price for men was higher than for women. Add to this the fights and drunk driving that occurred, and it's clear to see why some folks became so vehemently opposed to the opening of a dance hall in their area. In Platteville, a crowd of angry citizens surrounded the construction of a new dance hall being built just outside the city limits. Former State Senator John Grindell led the protesters in a chant, "The dance hall is a menace to the community morals!"

"WHERE THEY DRINK"
FROM THE SHEBOYGAN PRESS, 1929

Deprived of the saloon by the prohibition laws, Fond du Lac county citizens may drink near beer, sometimes something stronger, in their choice of more than 200 licensed places. Among the "wet parlors" in the county are the following:

The Bucket of Blood	Hollywood
The Broken Knuckle	Sunset Gardens
Pistol Pete's Place	Rustic Cave
The Muskrat House	Ole's Inn
Smokey Lang's Place	Crystal Palace
The Crows' Nest	Cedar Grove
The Rats' Nest	Riverside Inn
The Red Onion	The Idle Hour
The Diamond Merchant	Joe Kinker's Place

The Cinder Pit and Little Tia Juana have closed and are nothing but memories, but there are "plenty more."

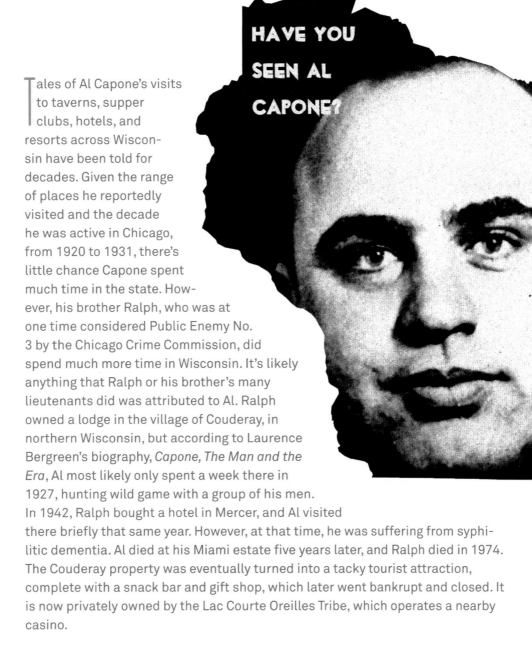

HAVE YOU SEEN AL CAPONE?

Tales of Al Capone's visits to taverns, supper clubs, hotels, and resorts across Wisconsin have been told for decades. Given the range of places he reportedly visited and the decade he was active in Chicago, from 1920 to 1931, there's little chance Capone spent much time in the state. However, his brother Ralph, who was at one time considered Public Enemy No. 3 by the Chicago Crime Commission, did spend much more time in Wisconsin. It's likely anything that Ralph or his brother's many lieutenants did was attributed to Al. Ralph owned a lodge in the village of Couderay, in northern Wisconsin, but according to Laurence Bergreen's biography, *Capone, The Man and the Era*, Al most likely only spent a week there in 1927, hunting wild game with a group of his men. In 1942, Ralph bought a hotel in Mercer, and Al visited there briefly that same year. However, at that time, he was suffering from syphilitic dementia. Al died at his Miami estate five years later, and Ralph died in 1974. The Couderay property was eventually turned into a tacky tourist attraction, complete with a snack bar and gift shop, which later went bankrupt and closed. It is now privately owned by the Lac Courte Oreilles Tribe, which operates a nearby casino.

Many of these remote roadhouses and dance halls, dens of evil that they were, became supper clubs when Prohibition was finally repealed in December 1933. While it's difficult to determine the precise moment the very first supper club appeared in Wisconsin, four places stand out as the earliest examples. The first of these became the very definition of supper club dining in Wisconsin. Despite the history of interstate rivalry—Bears vs. Packers, tollways vs. free highways, margarine vs. butter—it was just a stone's throw from the Illinois border.

Ray Radigan's

RAY RADIGAN'S Wonderful Food

Kenosha, Wisconsin

Raymond "Ray" Radigan was born in Kenosha in 1907. At the age of fourteen, he embarked on his restaurant career with a job as a busboy at the Lackner Restaurant in Waukegan, Illinois. After more than a decade of food service employment at other restaurants in Waukegan, he returned to Kenosha County and leased a small, four-room bungalow just north of the Illinois border, on a remote stretch of South Sheridan Road. The tiny roadhouse served hot meals, sandwiches, and home-brewed gin on the side. A slot machine kept the customers entertained, and a neon sign on the roof announced in red neon, "Ray Radigan's Wonderful Food."

In August 1934, Radigan married Wilma Kincaid. Wilma, along with Radigan's sister Rose, helped out at the roadhouse. As the business grew, he needed space to expand; in late 1935, Radigan purchased an old, white, two-story cottage about a half-mile north, on the opposite side of Sheridan Road. It was part of a farm owned by the estate of the recently deceased Edith Rockefeller McCormick, daughter of John D. Rockefeller and ex-wife of Harold F. McCormick. Work began to update the 133-year-old building with modern design elements, including indirect lighting.

In 1937, the grand reopening of his "inn," as he called it, featured the finest cocktails and an expanded dinner menu featuring a six-course steak dinner with shrimp cocktail for $1.25. Sandwiches were served until 12:30 a.m. A staff of twelve took care of the customers, and Radigan played the cordial host.

Ray Radigan
— Your Congenial Host

At the onset of the 1940s, Radigan was an expert self-promoter about to enjoy an era of rapid growth, but not without a bit of turbulence. In June 1940, around 2:30 a.m., as he and a few employees cleaned up after a long day, three men armed with revolvers and a shotgun entered through a back door and demanded money. One employee was pistol-whipped. Radigan, who was in another room, managed to escape upstairs to his office with the day's proceeds. After ransacking the first floor, the three gunmen fled empty-handed. From his upstairs window, Radigan fired five shots at the bandits; they returned fire with a volley of fifteen to twenty shots before they disappeared into the night. Unshaken by the attempted robbery, Radigan continued to expand the inn. By December 1940, construction of a second dining room was finished, and work on a new kitchen was also underway. New refrigeration units in the basement provided more cold storage and space to dry age beef. A new cook was hired to help the head chef and his assistant, an addition that enabled the kitchen to handle a larger number of diners. Two banquet rooms were also available for private parties of women's clubs, business dinners, and wedding receptions.

Upon returning from a seven-week vacation deep-sea fishing off the coast of Tampa, Radigan brought back a thirty-pound red snapper to serve at a staff dinner to celebrate. The partying went well into the wee hours, and Radigan was arrested for violating the state tavern closing hour law. He was fined twenty-five dollars and warned he would lose his liquor license for a second violation.

During World War II, Ray Radigan's was forced to close on Mondays due to the rationing of beef, butter, and other foods. In addition, gas rationing and the restrictions on the manufacture of rubber tires meant that the long drive out to Sheridan Road wasn't feasible for some customers. After the war ended, Ray Radigan's placed an ad in the local paper that jubilantly announced, "Yes! WE SAID STEAKS! Its [sic] been a long, long time since we've been able to serve you steaks like these—but now that we can, won't you visit us again!" Radigan's

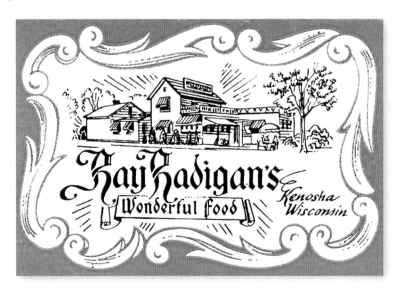

Ray Radigan's Wonderful Food Kenosha Wisconsin

SANDWICHES SERVED
TILL 12:30

A Nightcap at Radigan's
Where Prices are Reasonable

Come to Radigan's tonight after the show! You'll find the atmosphere most congenial, the drinks perfect, and the prices very moderate –she'll like Radigan's!

RAY RADIGAN
South Sheridan Rd.

1940

Yes!

WE SAID
STEAKS!

"Its been a long, long time"—since we've been able to serve you steaks like these— but now that we can, won't you visit us again!

Those Delicious, Delectable

STEAKS DONE IN THE "RADIGAN" STYLE
Served As You Like Them!

SEA FOOD • CHOPS • CHICKEN

The Original Home of "Wonderful Food"

RAY RADIGAN'S
South Sheridan Road   Phone Kenosha 9988

1946

also began to appeal to women meeting friends for lunch or cocktails during the day. It was known for serving healthy green salads, fresh fish, and seafood, in addition to the hearty dinners and late-night supper menu that kept the bar crowd happy. Unfortunately, in late 1947, Radigan's was cited again for remaining open after hours. After several court appearances, Radigan paid a stiff fine and was permitted to keep his liquor license.

During the 1950s, Ray Radigan's entered its heyday, which lasted for decades. By that time, Radigan had become something of a celebrity, the elder statesman of the supper club trend that was spreading across the nation. Continuous upgrades were added to improve the experience for customers, including a larger and newly redecorated cocktail lounge, air conditioning, and the installation of an acoustic ceiling so "patrons are not subjected to the annoying clank and clatter of dishes during their meal." In the fall of 1957, noisy plates were drowned out by televisions placed in the bar and dining rooms so customers were able to cheer the Milwaukee Braves as they beat the New York Yankees in the World Series.

In this era, family dinners were Radigan's new focus. Its "famous" platters offered choices of chicken, chops, shrimp, lobster, trout, scallops, or steak served alongside a generous relish tray of radishes, green onions, pickles, cottage cheese, corn relish, plus French-fried potatoes, and toast. The homemade cottage cheese, created by Radigan's mother Catherine, was another trademark dish. With its rave reviews, AAA-approved

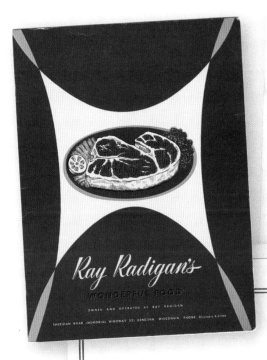

Ray Radigan's
menu, 1964

À La Carte

EACH OF THESE SELECTIONS GARNISHED WITH
French Fried Potatoes, Radishes, Pickles, Green Onions
Cottage Cheese, Hot Rolls and Tossed Salad

Pork Chop Plate	$2.50	Broiled Pork Chops	$3.25
Broiled Doubled Lamb Chop (1) ½ Lb.	$3.25	Ray's Special Steak Sandwich	$3.50
		Shrimp de Jonghe	$3.25
Chopped Sirloin Steak with Mushroom Sauce	$2.90	Ham Steak, Center Cut, with Glazed Pineapple	$3.25
French Fried Shrimp Platter	$3.00	Lobster a la Newberg	$3.50
French Fried Scallop Platter	$2.90	Broiled Double Lamb Chops (2) 1¼ Lb. to an order	$4.50
Fresh Chicken Livers with Mushrooms	$3.00	Lobster Thermidor	$3.75
1/2 Chicken Pan-Fried in Butter	$2.90	Our Famous Lobster Tail Platter	$5.00
Barbecued Baby Back Ribs	$3.40	Ray's Famous Prime Tenderloin Steak	$4.75
		T-Bone Steak	$5.50
		Prime Strip Sirloin Steak (Boneless) 1¼ Lb.	$5.50

RAY'S FAMOUS T-BONE STEAK SANDWICH
2 LB. PRIME BLUE RIBBON STEER
French Fried Potatoes, Iced Relish Tray, Bean Salad
Cottage Cheese, Hot Rolls and Tossed Salad $5.50

All of our meats are U. S. Prime

Deluxe Dinner
Served from 2:30 until 10:30 P.M. — Sundays from 12 Noon until 10:30 P.M.

FRESH SHRIMP COCKTAIL   ICED FRESH RELISH TRAY   CHILLED TOMATO JUICE
HOMEMADE SOUP   KIDNEY BEAN SALAD
COTTAGE CHEESE WITH CHIVES   SPRING SALAD
GARDEN VEGETABLES

Pork Chops	$4.00	Shrimp de Jonghe	$4.25
Barbecued Baby Back Ribs	$4.50	Our Famous Lobster Tail Dinner	
French Fried Scallops - Tartar Sauce	$3.90	1 Lb. with Drawn Butter	$6.00
French Fried Shrimp - Tartar Sauce	$4.00	Lobster Thermidor	$4.75
Fresh Chicken Livers and Mushrooms	$4.25	Lamb Chops	$5.50
Chicken, Half	$4.40	Tenderloin Steak	$5.75
Ham Steak, Center Cut, with Glazed Pineapple	$4.25	T-Bone Steak Dinner	$6.50
Lobster a la Newberg	$4.50	Boneless Strip Sirloin 1¼ Lbs.	$6.50

● Our 31st Year ●

NOT RESPONSIBLE FOR LOST ARTICLES   Service charge of 75¢ per person when meal is not ordered.
Take Home a Pint of Our Famous Cottage Cheese   .75

FRESH CALVES LIVER & BACON *3⁵⁰*

Broiled Bermuda Onion

Served Well Garnished With

Radishes - Onions - Relish

Cottage Cheese

Potatoes of the Day

Salad Bowl - Choice of Dressing

Hot Rolls

DE LUXE DINNER *4⁵⁰*

Served with all the trimmings

SPECIAL FOR TODAY

BROILED WHITE FISH . . . *3²⁵*

Served Well Garnished With

Radishes - Onions - Relish

Cottage Cheese - Hot Rolls

French Fried Potatoes

DE LUXE DINNER *4²⁵*

Served with all the trimmings

Ray Radigan's specials menus, 1964

status, and recommendations from Duncan Hines and other travel publications, "Ray Radigan's—Original Home of Wonderful Food" became known nationwide. A week-long twenty-fifth-anniversary celebration in September of 1958 featured an open house, free *hors d'oeuvres*, and complimentary champagne served from a fountain.

By the 1960s, Ray Radigan's was still *the* place to dine, despite the increasing competition not only in nearby Kenosha but in Chicago and Milwaukee as well. Celebrities including Waukegan native Jack Benny, Bob Hope, Muhammad Ali, and Carol Burnett visited to dine on Lake Superior whitefish and steak sandwiches. Chicago Mayor Richard J. Daley sometimes brought his day's catch from Lake Michigan to be prepared for dinner.

Radigan experimented briefly with fast food with Raymond's Drive-In, located on Douglas Avenue in Racine. The menu featured fifteen-cent hamburgers, twenty-cent hot dogs, and something called "Full Meal in a Bag . . . In a Minute" for forty-seven cents. His interest in the drive-in faded after a few years. It was sold in 1965 and is now DeRango's Pizza.

In 1971, Radigan's son, Michael, who had worked at the restaurant in his youth, returned to help run the business after he'd earned an MBA at Michigan State University. He eventually became co-owner with his father, and when Ray passed away in February 1994, Michael became the sole owner. For the time being, the two continued to work on making the supper club a success. In January of 1979,

Ray received a commendation from Kenosha Mayor Paul Saftig for his "ultimate aim of providing the connoisseur with sensitive and discriminating tastes."

In September of 1983, Radigan's celebrated its fiftieth year with a lavish party for 150 guests. Ray and his wife Wilma also celebrated their forty-ninth wedding anniversary and partnership in the business. While Michael was busy with the day-to-day operation of his father's place, he still managed to find the time to partner with his friend and former Radigan's employee Randy Ortloff to open Radigan's Taste of Wisconsin in May 1989. Located off I-94 on Highway 50, it featured the state's food products and dishes served from a huge, 3,000-square-foot kitchen. Despite its popularity, it closed in spring 2003 and was later sold to restauranteur Louis Tricoli for $1.15 million. After an extensive renovation, it reopened in December of the same year as The Birchwood Grill. It is still in operation today.

As Ray Radigan's continued into the new century, supper clubs faced tremendous pressure from chain restaurants. The economic crash of 2007 was a blow to all businesses, but especially small, independently owned establishments like family-owned supper clubs. Diners stopped spending as much on expensive meals, and their tastes and diet changed as well.

In 2012, Michael hired his daughter Mary as head chef. She put her unique culinary experience to use in crafting new menu items that included Thai coconut soup, Vietnamese pork ribs, tempura-fried Egyptian spring onions, and roasted bone marrow. "I don't want to lose the supper club feel, because I like it, it is fun," Mary said. "But at the same time, bringing a new flair and twist to it, I think, is very important." Another change included a controversial charge for the normally complimentary relish tray, which was met with disapproval from some long-time customers.

On Wednesday, May 27, 2015, patrons who arrived at Ray Radigan's were surprised to find a notice on the front door, printed in bold black letters:

> *On behalf of the Radigan family and staff...I would like to say THANK YOU*
> *to all of our loyal customers, past and present.*
> *Ray Radigan's will not reopen in the near future.*
> *AGAIN THANK YOU FOR ALL YOUR PAST AND PRESENT SUPPORT!*

The sudden closing of Ray Radigan's after eighty-two years was a shock to the loyal customers, the local community, and fans of Wisconsin supper clubs. When asked by a reporter from the *Kenosha News* about the closing, Michael Radigan said, "Maybe food like this has gone out of style. But it was high quality. We should have continued to have people lined up out the door." The property was sold in December 2016 for $130,000 and, as of this writing, the building sits unused.

The Turk's Inn

The story of The Turk's Inn begins in the 1920s when George and Isabella Gogian, a young Armenian couple living in Istanbul, Turkey, immigrated to Philadelphia, Pennsylvania. George was a chocolatier by trade, and he opened a small candy shop shortly after he arrived. Initially, it did well, but when the Depression wiped out the business, George headed west to St. Paul, Minnesota, to live with relatives. He found work as a waiter in a Hayward, Wisconsin, roadhouse called the Aladdin. When the Aladdin closed in 1934, he rented a tavern in town and started selling food, calling the place George's The Turk's Inn. In May of 1938, he purchased a small parcel of land next to the Namekagon River, three miles northeast of Hayward, and built a restaurant with living quarters on the second floor. He called it The Turk's Inn, and he and Isabella, who was known as "Mom," served an array of traditional Turkish dishes of beef and lamb along with steaks for the less adventurous eater. George's philosophy of dining was printed on the menus:

George "The Turk" Gogian

COURTESY OF VARUN KATARIA

The art of cooking is an art to be proud of; it is the soul of festivity at all times and to all ages. We Americans are prone to forget...that eating should be an unhurried pleasure, not a task to get over with quickly. Therefore, at least once a day, preferably in the cool and quiet of the evening, one should throw all care to the winds, relax completely, and dine leisurely and well.

—Salaam Alaikum
[in Arabic, "peace be upon you"]

Tom Shuman, a family friend of the Gogians, recalled going to The Turk's Inn with his parents and grandparents in the 1940s and '50s: "The food was

George and Isabella, 1934 COURTESY OF VARUN KATARIA

out of this world. At that time there weren't many nightclubs around and it was one of the highlights that they had such great food. George was a very vibrant person. He would remember names, knew what they drank. He was a short guy, maybe five-feet, or four-eleven, but very charismatic. I can still hear his laugh."

The decor in the Harem Lounge and Kismet Dining Room was a mix of Turkish art and Middle Eastern tchotchkes that George and Mom brought back from trips abroad. A collection of exotic birds roamed the grounds outside, and belly dancers, backed by Turkish musicians, entertained the diners. One of the belly dancers was the Gogians' daughter Marge, who eventually left to attend school in New York, where she became a fashion model and designer.

By the late 1950s, the inn attracted customers from around the country who had heard about The Turk and his delicious food. John F. Kennedy toured the state during the 1960 primary and is said to have stopped by, as did many other celebrities over the years.

"The Gogians were very respectful of the US flag," recalls Shuman. "During World War II, soldiers that came home on furlough could go to Turk's and everything was paid for. George took marvelous care of them." Gogian also helped his relatives immigrate to the US and paid for their educations.

In the 1960s, when Marge was in her thirties, her father requested that she return home to help out at the inn. She made the difficult decision to leave her career behind and return to Hayward. When George began to experience heart trouble, Marge's help was more important than ever. On Christmas Day, 1979, George died at the age of seventy-two. Marge stepped into her father's shoes as the gracious host. Customers enjoyed the special attention she gave them and that she made everyone feel like family when they visited.

As the Hayward area continued to attract visitors from all over for fishing, camping, skiing, and other recreation, The Turk's Inn continued to be a popular stop for hungry diners. However, as people cut back on dining out during the Great Recession, the inn began to show its age. Marge continued to work, despite her advanced age, and passed away at age eighty-five in February 2013. Tom Shuman said, "I kind of think the real person that made that business was her dad. His personality, his remembrance of things—I would say after George was gone, it was hard for Marge to keep up that end of it. Still, she made dining there a fond memory for everyone." It was only after Marge died that Shuman discovered that he was the executor of the estate. "In her will, which I had not seen before, the money that was left over, when everything was

The Turk's Inn menu,
circa 1960s

The Philosophy of Dining

The art of cooking is an art to be proud of; it is the soul of festivity at all times and to all ages. We Americans are prone to forget, in the ultra-rapidity of modern life — trying to crowd eighty seconds of toil into one minute's time — that eating should be an unhurried pleasure, not a task to get over with quickly. A dinner chosen according to one's needs, tastes, and moods, well prepared and well served, is a joy to all senses and an impelling incentive to sound sleep, good health, and long life. Therefore, at least once a day, preferably in the cool and quiet of the evening, one should throw all care to the winds, relax completely, and dine leisurely and well.

Salaam Alaikum
George Gogian

Hors D'Oeuvres & Relishes

TURK'S RELISH DISH	$1.75	BEOREK (Turkish Appetizer)	$ .75
SHRIMP COCKTAIL	2.00	TURKISH PICKLES	.35
TOMATO JUICE	.50	HOMEMADE SOUP	.40
ORANGE JUICE	.50	RIPE OLIVES	.40
STUFFED CELERY	.75	GREEN OLIVES	.40
CELERY	.40	PICKLED HERRING	1.00

Salads

TURKISH SALAD	$ .50
COLE SLAW	.40
TOMATO & LETTUCE	.50
SLICED TOMATO	.50
TOSSED SALAD	.50
ROQUEFORT DRESSING	.75

Desserts

PAKLAVA (Turkish Pastry)	$ .75
ICE CREAM	.35
SUNDAE	.40
HOT FUDGE SUNDAE	.50
CREME DE MENTHE PARFAIT	.85
TURKISH COFFEE	.75

The Turk's
Inn exterior,
2013

sold and disposed of, was supposed to go to scholarships for students in Hayward and Drummond areas. And it was also supposed to go to Armenian students that we could find in the Minneapolis-St. Paul area. What was left was $1.2 million, and right now we spend the earnings from that to provide between $30,000 and $40,000 for students to continue their schooling after high school. I think it's marvelous."

A second chapter opened for Turk's in 2017, when two Minneapolis natives, Varun Kataria and Tyler Erickson, purchased much of the decor and signage. With Tom Shuman's help, it was shipped to Brooklyn, where they opened their version of The Turk's Inn in the summer of 2019. As far as the new owners, Shuman said, "I always felt they were financially able to do what they have done. They have been very, very appreciative."

Word that a Wisconsin supper club was opening in the Bushwick neighborhood of Brooklyn became big news in the New York restaurant circles. Robert Simonson, a Wisconsin native, writing for *Grub Street*, said, "Curious New Yorkers should not go to the new Turk's thinking, 'Ah, so *this* is a Wisconsin supper club.' Rather, they should think that this is what the The Turk's Inn, specifically, was like." He enjoyed the food but pointed out it wasn't supper club cuisine. "That's a good thing, because here's the deal with Wisconsin supper clubs. They will never succeed, *as they are*, in cities like New York."

The Beverly Supper Club

What follows is the sad tale of a supper club that existed for less than three months. On December 22, 1934, a half-page ad in the Oshkosh Northwestern newspaper heralded the "Gala Opening" of The Beverly, "Oshkosh's Premier Supper Club." By March 2, 1935, the club had been raided by state treasury agents and shut down for selling untaxed liquor, most of which was moonshine.

During Prohibition, The Beverly was a soda parlor and restaurant called The Broadway; it had also been raided in March of 1934 for the very same reason. It was the first such raid in Oshkosh under the new laws governing the sale and distribution of liquor. During a confusing and contradictory series of license hearings before the city council, several men claimed ownership of both the Broadway and the Beverly, only to eventually be exposed as fronts for the real owner, a Milwaukee bootlegger named Norton Armstrong. Ultimately, it was Oshkosh's mayor, George F. Oaks, who put the kibosh on any further discussion over licensing. Not only did it mark the end of the Beverly Supper Club, but one year later, Armstrong was arrested in a raid on his moonshine operation in Shiocton and began to serve three-to-five years in the Wisconsin State Prison in Waupun. Moonshine was still being produced and sold after Prohibition ended due to the high taxes on alcohol at the time. It was more profitable—and dangerous—to make fake whiskey.

Riviera Supper Club

The origins of the Riviera Supper Club go back to 1932, when a former golf course clubhouse was transformed into the Clava Del Rio, or "Key to the River," and advertised as "Green Bay's Smartest Night Club." It was located three miles south of Green Bay and owned by Walter "Mickey" McMillin. The club offered three floor shows every evening, plus dining and dancing to the music of the Clava Del Rio Band. Nothing cost more than twenty-five cents, including the cover charge and soft drinks. For those who stayed home, the club's live music was often broadcast on the Appleton radio station WHBY.

When McMillin became seriously ill in the spring of 1934, Theodore "Pat" Selissen, who owned a tavern called Pat's Inn on Riverside Drive in Allouez, sold the bar to Ray Lefebvre and took over the lease of Clava Del Rio. He renovated the club and reopened it that fall as the Riviera. The nightclub again offered dining and dancing to Doc Scott and his Steamship Aquitania Orchestra. There were three different floor shows, a men's lounge, and the Horseshoe Bar, where the newly legal cocktails and highballs were poured.

Riviera opening night advertisement, 1934;
matchbook, 1947; advertisement, 1938

In June 1935, a fire tore through the club and the second-floor apartment where Selissen and his wife Florence lived. They survived, but the building was destroyed. A few months later, he purchased and renovated the spacious former home of Dr. Robert E. Minahan on Nicolet Drive, northeast of Green Bay. Situated on several wooded acres, it was a peaceful setting and offered a view of the bay. Opening night for the new Riviera Supper Club was Friday, November 15, 1934. Inside, customers found comfortable cocktail rooms, a club buffet bar made in Oshkosh by Robert Brand & Sons, and a cozy fireplace room. Shore suppers, as they were called, were served inside at tables from afternoon until closing. Dinner choices included fresh Maine lobster, steaks, pork and lamb chops, fried chicken, and French-fried shrimp. Selissen decided not to have any music, dancing, or entertainment in order to maintain a "decorum of a home of character," like the famous inns of colonial times. Advertised as a "Fashion-able Supper Club," it was quite a success.

In 1942, Pat Selissen died at forty-nine after a short illness. Florence took over operations for five years and then sold the club in December 1947. Five years later, Pat's brother Joe Selissen bought the Riviera Supper Club for $56,000, and the family tradition continued. In May 1966, Selissen sold the property for $75,000 to Brown County for the development of the University of Wisconsin-Green Bay campus. The building sat unused for years and fell into serious disrepair. In the summer of 1970, it was burned by the Green Bay Fire Department as a training exercise. The property is now part of Communiversity Park.

Paul's Nautical Inn

STURGEON BAY • 1928 TO 1965

Located at 234 Kentucky Street, the building dates back to 1886, and it was formerly the Sturgeon Bay Hotel. Purchased in 1928 by Joseph Paul, it featured the Marine Tap Room with model ships and a variety of nautical items. In the 1930s, the inn offered live music and dancing during lunch and dinner. After Joseph's death, his brother William J. Paul, who built the Holiday Motel and owned the Nightingale Supper Club and Smith Lodge, took ownership of the Nautical Inn. His son Raymond later ran it until 1965, when he left to start the Carriage Inn in Green Bay. The Nautical Inn remains open today and features bar food, electronic dance music, and sports on big-screen TVs.

Paul's Nautical Inn
dining room and
exterior, 1968

Jake Skall's Colonial Wonder Bar

APPLETON • 1932 TO 1972

Owners Jake and Agnes Skall began selling fifteen-cent chicken dinners from a road-side stand in 1932. Within a year, they moved into the Colonial Inn on South Memorial Drive, and installed a bar, back bar, and settee booths made by Robert Brand & Sons. They changed the name to Skall's Colonial Wonder Bar, and it became one of the Fox Valley's outstanding dining places, drawing customers from all over the country with its cuisine. Sons Donald and Russell both worked there after attending Notre Dame University. Russell became the manager-owner and later sold it to Green Bay restauranteur Clark Urban, who changed the name to the Ravine Supper Club.

Chapter 5

MILWAUKEE'S NIGHTCLUBS, SPEAKEASIES, AND ROADHOUSES

1920s AND 1930s

Roadhouse Nights, 1930

During Prohibition, there were speakeasies all over Milwaukee, in storefronts, former saloons, and even private homes. The infamous Dirty Helen, who ran a speakeasy called The Sun Flower Inn at 1806 West St. Paul Avenue, visited the city for the first time in 1926. In her book *Dirty Helen: A Zany, Wonderful, Unconventional Ex-Madam and Tavern Keeper Tells of Her Adventures, the Fascinating People She Has Known and the Exploits That Make Her a Living Legend*, she described what she saw:

"It would have been impossible to have counted the speakeasies and bordellos. There were at least 300 speaks in the Third Ward alone." At the time, the Third Ward was known as "Little Italy" and was run by brothers Giovanni (Pete) and Angelo Guardalabene, whose late father Vito was the first known head of the Milwaukee La Cosa Nostra and "The King of Little Italy." Pete was the "Prince of the Third Ward," and his Monte Carlo Café was a front for various Mob-related operations, including bootlegging. As a result, it was a frequent target of federal agents. The influence of the Mob, under the direction of the Chicago Outfit, was felt for decades in many of Milwaukee's bars, restaurants, supper clubs, and nightclubs. Bombings, murders, arson, and physical violence were used to intimidate club owners and often remained unsolved. But the Mob's control also meant Milwaukee club owners were protected, financed, and guaranteed to have something more intoxicating than ginger ale to serve during Prohibition.

"LOOK FOR ME HERE TONIGHT! ENJOY BETTER-TASTING HIGHBALLS FEEL THE DIFFERENCE TOMORROW!"

With the Big, 8-drink-size, 24 oz. bottles, you can enjoy the best for about 3 cents a highball. Also available in 12 oz. bottles.

White Rock's protective, natural mineral salts improve flavor of highballs, combat acidity...help keep you feeling fit next day

This *natural* mineral spring water is *super-charged* with a sparkle that stays to the end of your drink. White Rock costs a little more. But what a big *difference* it makes!

Compare White Rock with any ordinary sparkling water or club soda. Learn how it gives you better-tasting highballs...how it helps keep you feeling fit next day. Treat yourself to the best. Use White Rock tonight.

Try White Rock Sarsaparilla and Pale Dry Ginger Ale

Founded in 1871, White Rock mineral spring water from Waukesha became a household name by the 1930s. Greek goddess Psyche appeared on bottles and in ads promoting the supposed health benefits of the sparkling water with added lithium carbonate.

A CORNUCOPIA OF CLUBS

Besides Guardalabene's Monte Carlo and Miami Club, other Milwaukee night-spots that were open in the 1920s and '30s include The Inferno, The Jungles, Miami Gardens, Blue Heaven Club, The Aviator's Club, The Waiters Club, and a floating nightclub called The Steamship Mayflower.

Nightclub advertisements of the early to mid-1930s, including the Wagon Wheel Supper Club in La Crosse, Marine Club in Madison, and Alamo Club in Stiles, just north of Green Bay. Texas Guinan's appearance in Milwaukee in 1933 was one of her last before her death later that year.

Pick's Club Madrid

PICK'S CLUB MADRID, AMERICA'S MOST BEAUTIFUL CAFE, BLUEMOUND ROAD, MILWAUKEE

The western outskirts of Milwaukee, along Bluemound Road, were home to a number of roadhouses in the 1920s and '30s, including The Ship and Club Madrid, which were both owned by the "King of Nightlife" Sam Pick and his brother Joe. Their partnership began in 1917 when they purchased the Green Grill and Blue Chip roadhouses. In 1931 they opened Pick's Club Madrid, advertised as "America's Most Beautiful Café." It was also Waukesha County's largest nightspot, and notably the workplace of *Gone With The Wind* actress Hattie McDaniel. She was initially hired as an attendant in the ladies' room and later performed as a singer in the floor show before she found fame in Hollywood. In 1938, the Pick brothers were indicted by the Waukesha County prosecutor William J. McCauley for leasing rooms for gaming, the use of gambling devices, and for the sale of liquor after 1:00 a.m. The two were given suspended sentences, and they paid a fine of $1,000. In April 1953, an electrical fire began in one of the club's neon signs; it was fanned by winds up to twenty-five miles an hour and destroyed the building. Even worse, Joe Pick died

PICK'S CLUB MADRID, AMERICA'S MOST BEAUTIFUL CAFE, BLUEMOUND ROAD, MILWAUKEE

Pick's dollar dinner
advertisement, 1932

that same year. Sam Pick retired to Manitow-ish Waters, Wisconsin, and died in 1970, at the age of seventy-nine. Two stone gates and the remnants of a stone wall that marked the entrance to Club Madrid can still be seen at 12600 West Bluemound Road.

Wisconsin's post-Prohibition boom in supper clubs was most likely influenced by newspapers, radio, and Hollywood movies. O. O. McIntyre continued writing about New York's supper clubs in his column *New York Day By Day* until his death in 1938. *New York Daily Mirror* gossip columnist Walter Winchell perpetuated the snark by reporting in *his* syndicated column, *On Broadway*, "A newly formed exclusive supper club on 52nd Street had three customers the other night ... They can't figure why? ... Well, asparagus there costs $1.75." Local radio stations around Wisconsin often featured live broadcasts of the dance music from various clubs, and from 1934 to 1935, NBC aired *Jan Garber's Supper Club*, a prime-time variety show broadcast on Mondays. Bandleader Garber was dubbed "The Idol of the Airwaves." In 1937, NBC brought back the retitled *Supper Club* show, which featured "tunes which fit in with the early evening hour." Listeners in Wisconsin also enjoyed a 1938 broadcast featuring musician Bill Morgan, Bill Dodge and the Swing Seven, pianist Peggy Anderson, and Vic Fraser's orchestra playing several songs, including "Lovelight in the Starlight," "Stranger in Paree," "Hands Across the Table," "Dancing on the Ceiling," and "It's the Little Things That Count," among others.

But it was Hollywood that gave viewers a glimpse of the glamorous nightlife of New York's swanky nightspots, where dining out meant tuxedoes, expensive dresses, upscale food, dancing, and plenty of cocktails and champagne. Leo McCarey's screwball comedy, *The Awful Truth* (1937), starring Cary Grant and Irene Dunne, and *Mr. and Mrs. Smith*, a 1941 comedy directed by Alfred Hitchcock, are just two of many films of that era. In *Mr. and Mrs. Smith*, the actors visit The Florida Club and its overly crowded dance floor. Chuck (played by Jack Carson) and his date (Patricia Farr) order old-fashioneds and noisily eat celery from the relish tray. Meanwhile, David's (played by Robert Montgomery) blind date (Betty Compson) dines on roast pheasant, which she describes as, "Nothing but chicken, and a tough chicken at that . . . three bucks for this and a coupla French fries, what a racket."

Ralph Bellamy, Cary Grant, and Irene Dunne in *The Awful Truth* (1937)

Beginning in 1944, NBC's *Chesterfield Supper Club* Radio Show was broadcast five nights a week and featured singers Perry Como, Jo Stafford, and Peggy Lee.

Jack Carson, Betty Compson, Robert Montgomery, and Georgia Carroll at the Florida Club in *Mr. and Mrs. Smith* (1941). Note the relish tray in the foreground.

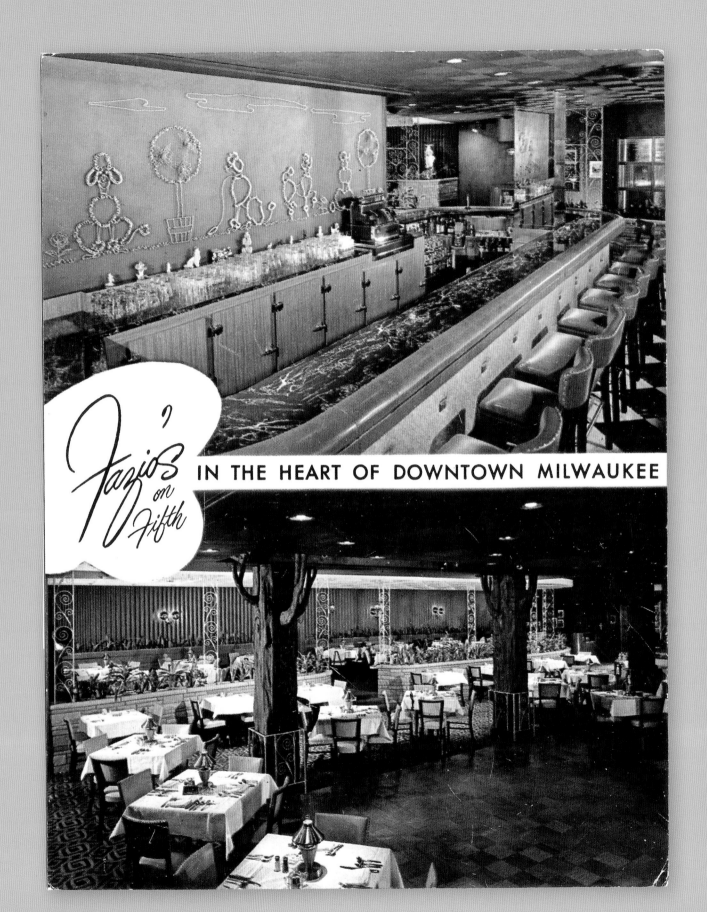

Fazio's on Fifth

IN THE HEART OF DOWNTOWN MILWAUKEE

Chapter 6

FAMOUS SUPPER CLUB FAMILIES

THE 1940s

As the Great Depression ended and the home front restrictions of World War II faded into history, the public wanted to experience a night out for dinner and dancing like their favorite movie stars did—at least once. The post-war boom meant that there were plenty of places offering good food, entertainment, and drinks. In the heart of downtown Milwaukee, there was one address that was home to no less than three supper clubs, a go-go bar, a disco, and a punk/new wave club over a period of forty-five years.

Tic Toc Club and Fazio's on Fifth

Jimmy Fazio's Supper Club

Situated between Wisconsin Avenue and Michigan Street, 634 North 5th Street was across from the main entrance to the Hotel Schroeder (later the Marc Plaza and now the Hilton Milwaukee Center). In 1937, it was home to the Tic Toc Tap, owned by Albert J. Tusa, a former fight promoter and notorious moonshiner, considered by federal agents as "the last of Wisconsin's bootleg barons." Tusa lived in what the newspapers called a "model home" on Woodburn Street in Whitefish Bay, but he was associated with some of the more notorious figures in Milwaukee's Little Italy, including Pete and

Tic Toc Club postcard and marquee, circa 1950s

Jewel Box Revue advertisement, 1952; advertisement for comedy performances, 1949

Angelo Guardalabene. He was also a vice president of the Milwaukee County Italian American Alliance in 1932. Despite a $74,000 federal tax lien, liquor conspiracy, and hijacking charges, in 1933, Tusa opened The Vanity Café, located at 641 North 3rd Street, next to the Davidson Theater. The Vanity was a cabaret and featured dinner, floor shows, and afternoon tea dances.

Tusa sold the club after a couple of years and went into the wholesale liquor business. Unfortunately, some of that wholesale liquor was his own bootleg whiskey, produced and bottled in the basement of his home. It was discovered during a raid by federal agents in 1936. Incredibly, he still somehow managed to purchase the Tic Toc Tap a year later and turned it into a top-tier supper club. He changed the name to the Tic Toc Club and brought to its stage emerging local and national talent, including comedian Joey Bishop, comic vocalist Martha Raye, singer Patti Page, and a brash new comedian, Lenny Bruce, who was fired after his first 1948 appearance. ("I shall never forget the dry-eyed manner in which Al Tusa, that prince of good fellows, told me to get lost," Bruce later commented. "And the point is, I deserved it.") Bandleader and trumpeter Harry James stopped by to check out a promising, young accordionist from Milwaukee, Tommy Gumina. He hired Gumina on the spot.

Tusa was regarded as the first local club owner to bring top stars to the city and was known in show business circles as "The Milwaukee guy who pays the big salaries." In 1952, the Tic Toc hosted the *Jewel Box Revue*, the first traveling revue of female impersonators. It was quite novel for the time. The *Jewel Box Revue* proved so popular it was held over for a third week.

In the summer of 1953, Tusa held a Golden Jubilee Testimonial Dinner at the club for his friend Sophie Tucker, who was known as "The Last of the Red Hot Mamas." She was celebrating fifty years in show business, and in the past was always invited to the Tusa home for an Italian meal when she was in town. Around 1954, Tusa decided to move on and began negotiating with buyers interested in purchasing the Tic Toc. Among the interested parties were the Fazio brothers.

From the 1950s through the '70s, Milwaukee's nightlife was dominated by the Fazio family. They owned several restaurants and nightclubs, not only in Milwaukee but in Fort Lauderdale, Florida, as well. The Fazio story begins in 1912, with newly-wed Italian immigrants Angelo and Cona Fazio, who lived in an Italian working-class neighborhood on Milwaukee's lower east side. Around 1928 they opened a corner grocery store at 1601 North Jackson Street. They raised eight children in the upstairs living quarters: Louis, James (Jimmy), Angelo Jr., Anthony (Tony), Frank, John, Josephine, and Ann. Cona's flavorful Italian dinners were a neighborhood favorite, and in 1934, the store was expanded into Fazio's Restaurant and Cocktail Lounge; it was later changed to Fazio's on Jackson. The menu featured Cona's homemade spaghetti and ravioli, plus steak and fried chicken.

In 1942, Jimmy entered the restaurant business himself. He ran Fazio's on Jackson, and briefly renamed it Jimmy Fazio's on Jackson. He later took over operations at The Pump Room in the Miller Hotel, which he renamed Jimmy Fazio's Towne Room after the hotel was sold and became the Towne Hotel. Located at 723 North 3rd

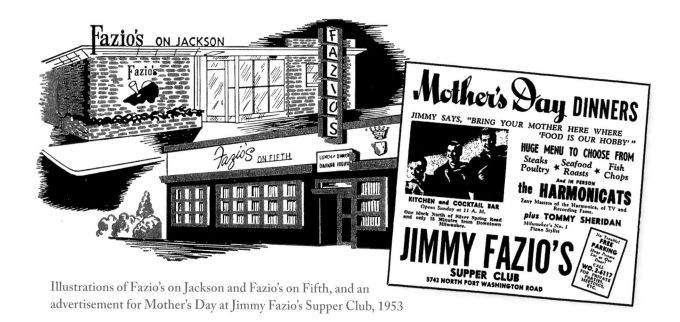

Illustrations of Fazio's on Jackson and Fazio's on Fifth, and an advertisement for Mother's Day at Jimmy Fazio's Supper Club, 1953

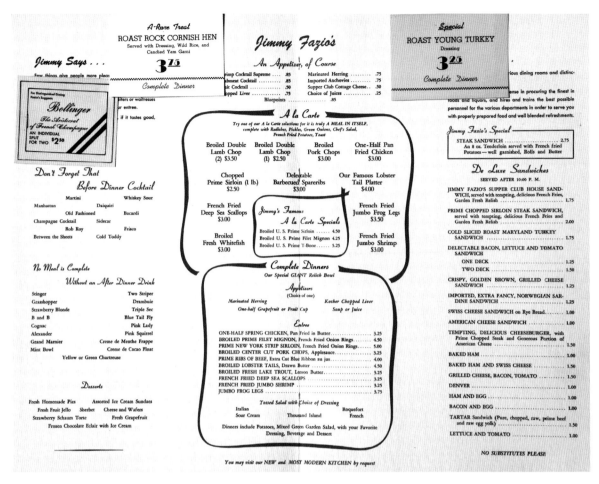

Jimmy Fazio's
Supper Club
menu, circa
1950s

Street, the supper club featured fine dining and live entertainment by "The Wizard of Waukesha," guitarist Les Paul.

In August of 1951, Jimmy sold his interest in the Towne Room and opened Jimmy Fazio's Supper Club in the former Arvay's Restaurant and Cocktail Lounge at 5743 North Port Washington Road in Glendale. The supper club quickly became a popular nightspot known for its prominent talent and excellent food, prepared by Swiss chef Sherby Babush. His menu featured steaks, chops, pan-fried chicken, frog legs, lake trout, and whitefish, along with the "Special GIANT Relish Bowl." A late-night sandwich menu included the Supper Club House Sandwich and the Tartar [sic], a Midwestern favorite made from chopped, raw, prime beef and raw egg yolk. As people dined, they were entertained by Tommy Sheridan, The Crew Cuts, Johnny Puleo and the Harmonica Gang, Dagmar, The Harmonicats, and Dick Contino.

"People are budgeted," said Jimmy shortly after the club opened. "They want something for their money, mainly food and fun and glamour. When they dine out, it's an occasion and we treat it as such." After not liking the way one band leader introduced an act, Jimmy decided to do it himself. He quickly downed three drinks, climbed up on stage, and opened with a couple of jokes before kicking things off with, "Show time!" The audience loved it, and it became his trademark.

In March of 1954, Cona, who had retired from cooking ten years earlier, passed away at the age of sixty-eight after a long stay at St. Luke's Hospital. The family was about to face an even more tragic year and a turning point for Jimmy and the supper club. The bad times began in February 1955, when Walter Ludwig, the forty-four-year-old owner of the Club Zircon in Cedarburg (and close friend and early promoter of Liberace), visited the supper club after hours to talk with Jimmy at the bar. Allegedly, Jimmy remarked that Ludwig wasn't a savvy enough operator to run a club as large as Fazio's; a heated argument ensued. According to testimony from witnesses, Ludwig fell and fractured his skull. He died at the hospital seven hours later. In a statement to Glendale police, Fazio said, "I told him he missed the boat . . . he was working while Liberace was making millions." Fazio also admitted that he hit Ludwig. However, after he refused to testify at the inquest by pleading the Fifth Amendment, a six-man jury ruled that Ludwig's death was accidental, and he did not die from a blow to the chin.

That same month, a federal tax lien was filed against Jimmy for $55,535 in cabaret taxes owed between January 1952 and December 1954. Earlier in the year, the state highway commission announced their plans to relocate Highway 141 (now I-43) in Glendale, and three buildings—Jimmy Fazio's Supper Club, The Farmer's Daughter dairy store, and Hanke's Tavern—were slated for demolition in January of 1956.

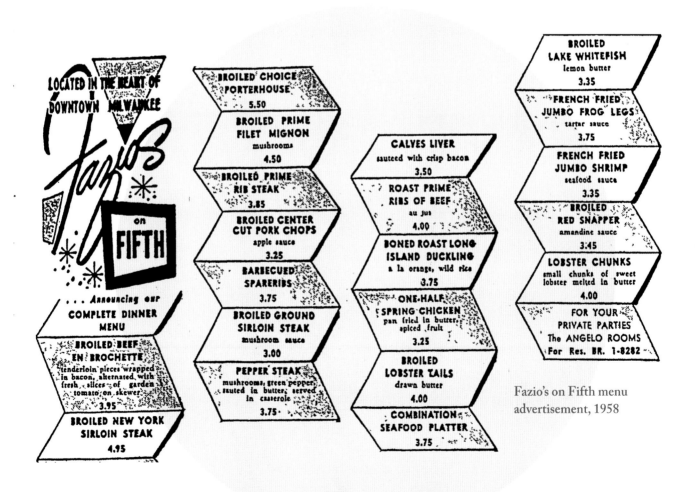

Fazio's on Fifth menu advertisement, 1958

Milwaukee County eventually paid $205,000 to Angelo, Sr. after it was revealed that he had purchased the title to the property for $60,000 in August of 1954. Jimmy only owned the business and fixtures, and as a result, the tax lien was not an issue in the sale of the club.

In the early morning hours of June 1, 1955, two explosions shook the Jackson Street neighborhood, blowing a huge hole in the wall of Fazio's restaurant and shattering the windows at several houses nearby. Investigators later found that two sticks of dynamite had been placed in a garbage can and set off one minute apart. Police investigated but claimed, "Nobody wants to say anything."

Frank Fazio, who lived next door, speculated, "Maybe somebody is jealous because we're so successful, and opening a spot downtown. Maybe somebody's got something against us. I don't know."

Angelo Jr. asked, "Why do they have to pick on us?"

Two days after the bombing, Angelo Sr. suffered a heart attack, which was blamed on the stress caused by the blast. In October, while visiting his daughter Josephine in Van Nuys, California, he suffered a stroke and died. He was sixty-seven.

As the family mourned again, Jimmy scheduled the final week of shows at his supper club; it featured former child actor and singer Bobby Breen. On New Year's

Demolition of 634 North 5th Street, Milwaukee, 1985

Jazz pianist Ike Cole (brother of Nat "King" Cole) at Fazio's on Fifth, 1969

Fazio's on Fifth exterior, 1962

Day, the club closed for good, and the contents were sold at auction ten days later. Fed up with the emotional and financial stress, Jimmy professed that he had "enough tough breaks in Milwaukee to last me a lifetime." His next act was to leave town and head to sunny Fort Lauderdale, Florida, where he eventually opened several supper clubs, including Jimmy Fazio's Restaurant and Lounge, the Town House, Jimmy Fazio's House of Prime Ribs, and the Fireside Steak House. Once again, Jimmy reveled in the attention of his patrons by performing as master of ceremonies.

The spot downtown that Frank Fazio speculated had sparked jealousy was the former Tic Toc Club on 5th Street. After seventeen years of running the Tic Toc, Al Tusa began negotiating with Jimmy and Frank Fazio to sell the club. However, the police investigation of the bombing at Fazio's on Jackson showed others were looking to acquire the Tic Toc, and they might have ties to the Chicago Mafia. After a nearly month-long investigation, Chief John Polcyn finally submitted his recommendation to the common council for a license for Frank Fazio to open Fazio's on Fifth. Frank, with help from his brother Tony, continued to book national and regional acts, like the singing group The Hilltoppers, comedian and impressionist Will Jordan, musician Ike Cole (brother of Nat "King" Cole), and singer June Valli. Actor John Carradine, who was appearing in a play at the Fred Miller Theatre on Oakland Avenue, stopped by one night and was persuaded to sing several songs for the delighted crowd. Frank saw Fazio's on Fifth as filling a void that pleased other businesses. "They're happy about it because downtown needs a good spot," he told reporters. "Can you name me one good spot there now?"

While there were quite a few notable places to eat and see a show in Milwaukee at the time, by the late 1960s and '70s, the area around Fazio's on Fifth was getting run down and seedy. Grand old movie houses screened X-rated films to pay the rent, and pawn shops and adult bookstores infiltrated empty storefronts. Suburban flight

A Broadway
revue at Fazio's
on Fifth, 1967

was killing what was left of downtown nightlife; the Fazios decided it was time to move on. "Nightclubs can no longer compete with the sets, color, and absolute top entertainment provided by television," Tony Fazio said. "Then the 1967 riots hit Milwaukee, and the local citizenry seems to have boycotted downtown . . . we had no choice but to sell out."

In April 1970, Eddie Carroll, who owned the Casino Steak House one block north on 5th Street, bought Fazio's on Fifth. Banking on a new beginning in a bigger location, plans for the renamed Eddie Carroll's Casino were to keep the lower-level piano bar open and possibly continue live entertainment on the main floor. However, after only a couple of years, Carroll, who also owned the Country Squire Supper Club in Muskego, moved the Casino to 3322 Sheridan Road in Kenosha.

The next tenant at 634 North 5th opened a quasi-strip club featuring go-go dancers all day, plus "Live Cabaret Dancing" and the piano bar. It later became a disco

Madison punk band, Appliances SFB,
at Starship, 1982 COURTESY OF JAMES PRINZ

Exterior of Starship, 1982

called Starship Encounters, run by George Baldwin. In 1980, his son Kenny, a talented drummer, opened Starship, a punk rock nightclub that served only drinks (and mostly beer at that). By this time, the club was showing its age. It looked rather beat up and neglected, which created the ideal atmosphere for the punk rock crowd. Cockroaches scurried across the bar as businessmen, slowly realizing that hookers no longer hung out there, gulped their drinks and hurried out. The club's walls were painted black, and various gig posters were tacked up over them. The walls of the bathrooms were covered in graffiti. After many legendary live performances over two tumultuous years (including one by the author's band, Couch Potatoes, later known as Couch Flambeau), Starship closed. In 1985, the City of Milwaukee demolished 634 North 5th, along with the rest of the buildings along Wisconsin Avenue between 4th and 5th Streets, citing future development. Many projects were proposed for the site, and many were blocked. Today, the site of one of Milwaukee's most historic supper clubs is a surface parking lot.

FROM SUPPER CLUB TO PUNK CLUB

Much like the Tic Toc and Fazio's on Fifth, Starship hosted many up-and-coming acts. Between-band entertainment was provided by a Gorgar pinball machine and a beloved jukebox loaded with the latest punk and new wave tunes ("Warm Leatherette" anyone?). The lineup of local and national acts that played at the Starship included:

- Black Flag
- Bush Tetras
- Captain Beefheart
- James Chance and the Contortions
- The Cramps
- The Damned
- Dead Boys
- D.O.A.
- Fear
- Flipper
- Lydia Lunch
- Pere Ubu
- Snakefinger
- Sun Ra
- The Troggs
- T.S.O.L.
- The Ventures
- The Waitresses
- X

Local bands included:
- Ama-Dots
- Appliances SFB
- Blackholes
- Buck Byron and the Little Seizures
- Paul Cebar
- Couch Potatoes
- Die Kreuzen
- The Haskels
- Locate Your Lips
- Lubricants
- Oil Tasters
- Plasticland
- Prosecutors
- Spooner
- Tense Experts
- Violent Femmes
- XCleavers

COURTESY OF GUY HOFFMAN

Hoffman House

Ishnala

HILL'S "ISHNALA" ON MIRROR LAKE, LAKE DELTON, WIS.

Hill's
Ishnala,
circa 1940s

Like the Fazios, another prominent family became a major influence in Wisconsin and beyond. The Hoffman brothers established a popular Midwestern supper club brand and saved what later became a landmark destination and one of the most well-known supper clubs in Wisconsin.

Their story begins in Madison, Wisconsin, where Fred Hoffman and his wife Florence raised nine boys—Jerry, Fran, Cy, Bob, Walt, Cos, Chuck, Bud, and Tommy. Fred owned a series of small grocery stores around Madison between 1915 and 1935. One Hoffman's Grocery, also known as F. J. Hoffman's, was located at 706 University Avenue, another was at 2136 Regent Street, and one was on Monroe Street by the Camp Randall football field, aptly named the Stadium Food Shop. Fred also briefly owned Hoffman's Potato Chip Shop in the 400 block of State Street. The Hoffman family lived on Van Buren Street in the Vilas neighborhood, not far from Lake Wingra.

In 1940, eight of the brothers—excluding Tommy, who was only eight years old—decided to open a restaurant and cocktail bar when Fred's health prevented him from working. They figured the business would "help them see their father through," as well as be profitable. At the time, Fran and Bob worked in a Madison lunchroom while attending classes at UW-Madison. The brothers applied for a food and liquor license but were forced to cancel their plans after the US entered World War II, because they anticipated they would soon be drafted. Indeed, all eight served in different branches of the service, and all but one returned. Bud was killed in action over New Ireland in the South Pacific on his birthday, February 14, 1944. He died the same day his parents were honored in a public ceremony at city hall to recognize their sons' service.

When the seven brothers reunited at the end of the war, they pooled their money, and in December of 1945, purchased an old shoe store at 514 Wilson Street, in what was considered the Skid Row area of Madison. It wasn't much, but it was all they were able to afford. The newly opened Hoffman House had room for forty-eight customers, and they took in twenty-eight dollars on their first day. Walter recalled, "We figured that by all of us working together, we could get a better hold on Old Man Opportunity."

The Hoffman House was open seven days a week, and live music was provided by Arnie Finsness on piano. In 1947, they began offering noon luncheons of steak, seafood, and club sandwiches; the special on Tuesdays was peel-and-eat shrimp with a homemade dipping sauce. The brothers began a major remodeling project in September that year to enlarge the dining area and add air conditioning. In February 1948, they formally opened four additional rooms: the Sky-Lite Room, the Chandelier Room, and the Llama Room, along with the private Goldwood Bar, all located on the second floor. A special Hoffman House show was broadcast on the WIBA radio station with interviews and music from the new dining rooms. The menu was revamped and included a special of whole brook trout served on a birch plank. The Hoffman House had become one of Madison's swankiest eating and drinking spots.

A profile published in the *Milwaukee Journal* in April 1949 detailed the brothers' success story and outlined their individual roles in the Hoffman House enterprise. Jerry was the oldest and oversaw the retail salad dressing line. Fran was an attorney who handled legal matters for the company; he also was a songwriter and occasionally played piano in the supper club's cocktail lounge. Cy was the general manager of the restaurant and affiliated companies; Bob serviced the equipment of the restaurant; Walt served as the genial host greeting the guests; Cos was the bookkeeper and custodian of the kitchen; Chuck was the chief bartender and occasional supper club photographer; and the youngest brother,

MAD CITY DINING IN 1945

The Hoffman Brothers' competition at the time included Crandall's On the Square at 13 East Main, DiSalvos at 810 Regent, Tenderloin Inn at 2438 Washington Avenue, Cuba Club at Middleton Road, Roman Inn at 46 North Park Street, College Inn at State & Henry at Johnson, Bunky's on Park and Regent, the Italian Village at 651 State Street, The White Manor (formerly the Miami Club) on Sherman Avenue, Jimmie's "The Ace of Places" 906 Regent, and Julian's Flame at 540 State.

'Eating, Family Style'

A relatively (pun intended) successful enterprise is Hoffman House in Madison. It is the restaurant of the eight Hoffman brothers, who are shown above in front of their photographs. Left to right are Jerome (Jerry), 35; Francis (Fran), 33; Cyril (Cy), 31; Frederick Robert (Bob), 29; Walter (Walter), 26; Cosmas (Cos), 24; Charles (Chuck), 22, and Thomas (Tommy), 17. The missing brother is Bud

(Sylvester), who was killed in the south Pacific on his birthday, Feb. 14, 1944, while flying his next to last bomber mission before returning to the United States. The restaurant idea sprouted in 1941 with

Fran and Bob, who were working in a campus lunchroom while attending the University of Wisconsin in Madison. Fran was chef, Bud was cashier, Cy was a salesman and agreed to join them. But war came and their plans were delayed. Bud was killed, but the other two were joined by their other brothers and Hoffman House became a reality in December of 1945.   —Journal Staff Photos by Angus McDougall

The eight Hoffman brothers, *Milwaukee Journal*, 1949

COURTESY OF BOB PROSSER

Tommy, pitched in on odd jobs after school. The images of all nine brothers, including Bud, were featured on the cover of the Hoffman House menus and matchbooks.

Two years later, another expansion brought the total seating capacity to 360 people. The brothers hosted an open house in October to unveil the new and expanded rooms, plus four new pianos, kitchens, walk-in coolers, cocktail bars, two new salad bars, and three coatrooms. The Paul Bunyan room had an active waterfall, a wishing well, and a colorful stone fireplace. The Gay Nineties Fun Room had a "horseless carriage" and replica "hoosegow," where people were able to pose for photos taken behind bars. The parking lot was also expanded, and a rear entrance with an awning was installed to protect customers from the weather. Dining and dancing were featured on Wednesdays, Fridays, and Saturdays with music by the Mainliners. A Swedish smorgasbord was featured on Sundays. The grand opening included a floor show by Chippewa Indian dancers from the Lac du Flambeau tribe in Iron County.

On June 18, 1953, Fred and Florence Hoffman were driving back to Wisconsin after spending two months at their new vacation home in Sarasota, Florida, when the car left the road and crashed outside of Gainesville. Fred, who was driving, was severely injured, and Florence was killed. She was sixty-six years old. In her honor, the Hoffman House was closed on Monday, June 22.

In August 1957, Fred Hoffman passed away at the age of seventy after suffering a heart attack at his home. The Hoffman House was closed for a day in his honor.

The Hoffman's next venture took them just over the Illinois border, where the Hoffman House of Rockford was opened in early 1958. It was managed by Walt. Located at 3703 East State Street, it was designed in a western motif with an open-hearth cookery as the centerpiece in the Prairie Schooner dining room. The Palomino Lounge featured a console-type bar and nightly live music.

In January 1959, Madison's Chief of Police, Bruce Weatherly, drove his squad car into the path of an oncoming oil truck. The impact crushed his police cruiser and pushed it seventy feet down the road. Incredibly, Weatherly wasn't seriously hurt, but the accident prompted an investigation by a City Council committee after it was revealed that he had spent several hours in the bar at the Hoffman House while on duty. A bartender testified that Weatherly was served as many as twelve or more old-fashioneds, and multiple witnesses testified that the chief appeared drunk before he got into his squad car. Testimony was also presented that a bar manager had instructed the bartender to water down some of the drinks being served to Weatherly. Cy and Chuck were called as witnesses, and Fran acted as their attorney. Months later, when the Hoffman House's Class B license was up for renewal, Alderman Harold E. Rohr of the Fourteenth Ward was against granting a license because "it was shown that the Hoffman House served the police chief watered drinks and charged full price for them." Rohr noted it wasn't proper procedure and that the customer should have been refused service altogether. Even so, the license was granted, and Weatherly was ultimately fired after the investigation. In a bizarre twist, old-fashioneds had been mentioned so many times during the inquest, including during testimony about the recipe the Hoffman House used (whiskey, not brandy), that the drink became Madison's most requested and best-known cocktail.

Fran had discovered a unique salad dressing recipe in Bavaria during World War II and served it at the Hoffman House. Customers enjoyed it so much, they wanted some to take home. In 1948, the Hoffman brothers began to market their own line of sauces in grocery stores. The Hoffman House Sauce Company's first batches were bottled in the basement of the supper club. The bottles were initially sold as salad dressing, but the brothers started calling it a sauce when customers shared with them how they incorporated it into their meals. After a boom in sales, the bottling operation moved to 124 Butler Street, and by 1953, a modern new plant was opened at 2620 East Washington Avenue that turned out sixty jars per minute. Eventually, twelve different dressings and sauces were produced and sold in grocery stores in the Midwest and eastern states. In 1962, the Hoffman House Sauce Company went public, and in the summer of 1964, it was sold to Dean Foods, based in Franklin Park, Illinois. For years, the Hoffman House Shrimp & Seafood Sauce was the most popular of all the sauces.

ASK YOUR GROCER
HOFFMAN HOUSE *SAUCE*
"The All Purpose Dressing"

• *MEATS*
• *SALADS*
• *SEA FOODS*
• *CHEESE*

America's favorite sauce. . . sold In food stores everywhere . . . originated at the famous Hoffman House Supper Club in Madison, Wisconsin. Visit the Unique Hoffman House anytime. It's a "Drive Worth Taking".

"Every House needs Hoffman House"

HOFFMAN
HOUSE
DINNER CLUB

HOFFMAN HOUSE SAUCES & DRESSINGS ORIGINATED HERE

Hoffman
House menu,
circa 1950s

"Grandma Rogers"

OUR expert baker

Grandma Rogers bakes all
Hoffman House Desserts and
Pastries in Our Own
Bake Shop

Featuring | Strawberry Chiffon Pie
Black Bottom Pie
Homemade Blueberry Muffins

**Your Waitress Will Display the
Dessert Tray**

FREE PARKING

WOULD YOU HELP US!

Dining space is most always available despite the filled appearance of our parking lots which are still too small, even after enlargements.

So — in the evening, please allow our parking attendant to park your car in our nearby lots.

Drive in and say, "Park it, please!"

Table D'Hote Dinners

APPETIZERS

Fruit Juices — Our Home Soups — Consomme

LAZY SUSAN

with

Cheese Compote	Iced Relishes	Marinated Herring
Chicken Liver Spread	Spiced Crab Apple	Cream Cheese & Chives

SALADS

Greens Salad Bowl   Crisp Heart of Lettuce
choice of dressings from table decanters
crumbled Roquefort 25 cents extra

HOME STYLE ROAST CHICKEN — featured		2.90
FANCY CHICKEN LIVERS EN BACON		2.50
TENDERLOIN BEEF BROCHETTE		3.00
BROILED BABY BEEF TENDERLOIN		3.60
TOP SIRLOIN FOR TWO	TWO	6.90
	ONE	3.50
ROAST PRIME RIB O' BEEF — House Special		3.95
NEW YORK SIRLOIN — featured		4.35
PREMIUM AGED BEEF FILET MIGNON		3.95
BROILED T-BONE — Porterhouse Cut		4.60
BROILED CALVES LIVER EN BACON		2.75
SUPPER CLUB BEEF TENDERLOIN		2.90

SPECKLED BROWN TROUT — Caught live in our pool	
Broiled Immediately	3.75
FISHERMAN'S PLATTER — ON PLANK	
Six Varieties of Sea Food—Friday Only	3.75
AFRICAN LOBSTER TAIL — House Special	3.60
GULF COAST DEEP FRIED SCALLOPS	
Friday Only	2.75
SHRIMP FROM NEW ORLEANS	2.90
FILLET LAND O' LAKES PIKE	2.75

Baked Potato with Cheese and Chive Sauce or Hollandaise Sauce
Hash Browns   Parsley Buttered   French Fries
or
Vegetable of the Day
Coffee, Tea, Milk   Home Baked Rolls   Butter   Mints

In September of 1960, the Hoffman House on Wilson Street closed for a complete rebuilding and introduced a new theme. It was advertised as "San Francisco comes to Madison . . . the ultimate in gracious dining in the finest SF tradition." Two months later, the new and completely redesigned Hoffman House was open for business. It now featured an open-hearth grill in the former Gay Nineties Room, along with a salad bar. Other changes included the relocation of the bar and the installation of a new kitchen. Prime rib was always a popular dish, and it was noted that nearly twenty tons of it were served in one year at the Madison location alone.

1964 saw the release of *The Hoffman House Presents: An Evening with "Barney" Gugel* on the Cuca label from Sauk City, Wisconsin. Its twelve tracks featured standards like "When the Saints Go Marching In," "Sweet Georgia Brown," and "Carolina in the Morning," with Gugel on organ, accordion, and vocals. He was a regular performer at the Hoffman House in Madison and Rockford, and the liner notes on the album give an idea of what people can expect:

Barney Gugel
LP, 1964
COURTESY OF
BOB PROSSER

> "Barney is an absolute NUT. The selections are those most enjoyed by his audiences from Coast to Coast, Alaska, and the Hoffman House Dinner Clubs. CAUTION PLEASE: If you are looking for soothing, relaxing moments, AN EVENING with BARNEY GUGEL is not for you, sorry."

1965 marked a major turning point for the Hoffman brothers. In May, a third Hoffman House opened on the east side of Madison inside a motel called Midway Motor Lodge. The main dining room featured a huge spreading oak tree, the largest ever inside a building at the time. The partnership between the two companies was the first of several locations around the Midwest. Not to be left out, the Wilson Street location transformed into the Hoffman House Stage Door, a club and café with dancing and entertainment nightly. New menu items included a large Caesar salad served on a ten-inch plate and steaks smothered in crispy onion rings. Plans were also in the works to open a fourth Hoffman House in the Hilldale Shopping Center on the west side of Madison. It was expected to be triple the size of the downtown property.

Further development was in store in 1966 as the Hoffman House West opened in the Hilldale complex, and construction was underway on a fifth Hoffman House at Madison's Municipal Airport, along with a cocktail lounge, coffee shop, and newsstand. The biggest change, however, was the closing of the first location on Wilson Street after twenty years. It reopened under new ownership in April as the Beef Chateau, then became Lombardo's, a discotheque with go-go dancers, then the Unlisted Number nightclub, then Rudy's 007. The high turnover was evidence that the

OUR DINNERS FEATURE

a special STAGE DOOR salad created by Caesar with croutons, flakes of Italian cheese, three species of lettuce and…zesty Caesar dressing

FIVE STEAKS…   AND…

All steaks are smothered with fabulous onion rings!

filet mignon	3.95	broiled pork chops (two)	3.25
boneless Delmonico	3.75	baked red snapper	3.75
T-bone	3.95	lobster lagustino sauté butter	3.75
New York strip sirloin	3.95	New Orleans shrimp	3.50

FRIDAY

baby beef tenderloin	3.75
fisherman's basket with six varieties of seafood	3.85
shrimp basket	2.75

STAGE DOOR PLATTERS served noon and night

bar-b-q ribs   2.50
• baby back ribs with RIB FIXIN'
• cup of soup • onion ring • beverage

tenderloin steak 7 oz.   2.50
〖served open face〗
• french fried onion rings • cup of soup • beverage

THE STAGE DOOR LUNCHEONS

offers a noon lunch of changing soups, a luncheon salad, five open face sandwich plates and two hot lunches at one price

Rube's Reuben

chicken ala king

tenderloin tip casserole

STAGE DOOR SPECIAL
ham and turkey on English muffin topped with crumbled blue cheese and dressing

king crabmeat

turkey rarebit

hamburger in skillet

1.50

DANCING NIGHTLY FROM 9:00

SHOWS START AT_____PM

CLOSED ON SUNDAY

Stage Door menu, 1965 COURTESY OF BOB PROSSER

neighborhood had fallen onto hard times and influenced the brothers' decision to head towards the suburbs. (In 1983, The Essen Haus, owned by Bob and Gail Worm, opened in the former Hoffman House property and its success helped revitalize the neighborhood.)

When Hoffman House marked its thirtieth anniversary in 1976, there were more than 1,200 employees at eleven Hoffman House restaurants, including the lakeside supper club called Ishnala, which the brothers had purchased in 1953. As the era of corporate mega-mergers was just getting started, the Green Giant corporation purchased the Hoffman Houses, including Ishnala, in 1976, for approximately $6 million in stock, adding to the several Henrici's restaurants they already owned in Illinois. Two years later, Pillsbury bought Green Giant and immediately tried to sell off the restaurants. In 1981, Richard Seal, president of the office that was managing the Hoffman Houses and Henrici's, formed an investment group to acquire six restaurants from Pillsbury, including the Hoffman Houses in Madison, Janesville, and Rockford, plus Ishnala and two Henrici's in Chicago. Midway Motor Lodges bought nine Hoffman Houses (including the East Madison location) and the right to use the name in future expansions. Individual franchisers purchased the remaining restaurants.

The Ishnala Supper Club might have just been a blip on the Wisconsin dining scene if it weren't for the foresight of the Hoffman brothers. Situated on a hill in Lake Delton overlooking Mirror Lake, Ishnala was once a creek-side meeting place for the native Winnebago tribe; it later became a fur trading hut in the early 1800s. Horace

PET FOOD

Ask your waitress for our Soil-proof bag in which to put meat gleanings from your table or from our kitchens.

A Hoffman House doggie bag note.
COURTESY OF BOB PROSSER

The 1940s-era fireplace can still be viewed at Ishnala today.

HILL'S "ISHNALA" ON MIRROR LAKE, LAKE DELTON, WIS.

"ISHNALA" ON MIRROR LAKE, LAKE DELTON, WIS.

Hill's Ishnala dining room in 1940s, now part of the upper seating area

LaBar installed a dam on Dell Creek in 1860 for his flour mill (later renamed Timme's Mill), which created the placid Mirror Lake. In 1909, the original fur trading post was transformed into the log cabin summer home of a Shakespearian Broadway actor named Coleman. Decades later, a naval officer by the name of Harold J. Hill, who was the former owner of the Warren Hotel in Baraboo, purchased the five-acre property in 1946 and converted the cabin into a small candlelight supper club called Hill's Ishnala. Only open between May and October, Hill's offered Lake Michigan trout, fried Biloxi shrimp, fried scallops, lobster ala Newburg, Louisiana Frog Legs, Long Island Duck, roast prime rib, ham steak, country-style fried chicken, broiled sirloin steak, broiled filet mignon, or porterhouse steak—all priced between two and three dollars. Madison's *Capital Times* columnist Roundy Coughlin described Hill's Ishnala in his typically peculiar syntax: "It is the most beautiful place in Wisconsin you ought to see it brother what a layout. It is back in the woods I'm telling you something." After only two years, however, Hill was suddenly faced with finding a buyer or having to close the supper club; during the winter, he had returned to service in Miami, and the navy decided he needed to be there full-time. A Baraboo Chevrolet dealer and local character named E. E. Berkley scooped up the remote resort and managed to keep it open while he looked for a buyer. He also built a new structure for his living quarters, which became known as Berkley's Cabin.

For years, visitors have been told that Ishnala is a Winnebago Indian name meaning "By itself alone." While that translation made its first appearance in 1960, no one is sure where it originated or if it is, indeed, correct. It's quite possible that it was a corruption or an appropriation of "Alone in All its Greatness," a slogan used by the Ringling Brothers Circus whose headquarters were in nearby Baraboo.

In August 1953, the Hoffman brothers made a deal with Berkley to purchase Ishnala, making it their second restaurant. That winter, the log cabin was remodeled and enlarged. Seventeen picture windows facing Mirror Lake were added, and seven tall Norway pines were planted in the floor of the dining room. When Hoffman's Ishnala opened for the season in May of 1954, it boasted food, cocktails, and dancing, along with swimming and scenic boat trips on the lake. Waitresses wore tight, red, belted dresses with beaded headbands with one tall feather sticking out. A piano player and female vocalist provided the live entertainment. Further improvement followed the next year as a bi-level deck that overlooked the lake was added to what the Hoffmans called a "Beach Supper Club." The 1956 season was shortened by a week in order for major renovations to take place, as one hundred tons of flagstone were used for the foundation of a new Arrowhead bar. Outdoor decks, an open-air veranda bar, and the Patio Club room used for games and relaxation were also added on a second level. Another new feature was the Top O' The Pines Room on the top floor of the building, which

Cliff Supper Club
● Mirror Lake near the Dells

ISHNALA is an Indian name meaning "by itself alone", a point of rock extending into the clear and peaceful waters of Mirror Lake. ISHNALA was a red man trading post with Winnebago-made birch canoes paddled to its door.

Only foot paths and water ways connected ISHNALA to civilization until purchased by Coleman's of Broadway Fame. After World War 2, new owners opened its doors to the public as a Candlelight Supper Club. With some repairs the original rustic charm has been magnificently maintained...and now NEWLY EXPANDED.

WINTER WONDERLAND DAYS
will be commenced in 1960
● Skating to music
● Short run Tobogganing
● Holiday Food

Charter a bus to ISHNALA . . .
A TRIP WORTH TAKING

"SEVEN TALL PINE TREES GROW THROUGH THE FLOOR AND CEILING"

HOFFMAN HOUSE

Ishnala

on Mirror Lake
LAKE DELTON, WIS

● FOOD & COCKTAILS
● SWIMMING & DANCING
● SCENIC BOAT TRIPS
● PRIVATE PARTIES

Spend The Day at Beautiful Ishnala

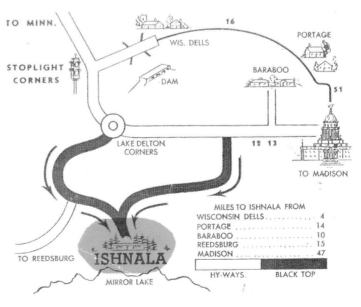

TO MINN.   16   PORTAGE
WIS. DELLS
STOPLIGHT CORNERS   BARABOO   51
DAM
12 13
LAKE DELTON CORNERS   TO MADISON

MILES TO ISHNALA FROM
WISCONSIN DELLS 4
PORTAGE 14
BARABOO 10
REEDSBURG 15
MADISON 47
HY-WAYS.   BLACK TOP

TO REEDSBURG   ISHNALA
MIRROR LAKE

had been used as living quarters. Standing more than sixty feet above the ground, the room offered stunning views of Mirror Lake and the spectacular sunsets over the pine trees. However, three weeks before the new renovations were about to be unveiled, a five-acre forest fire threatened to burn down Ishnala. Flames got as close as the parking lot before firefighter crews from the Wisconsin Dells, Lake Delton, and Reedsburg extinguished the blaze. The 1957 season opened on May 26, and Cy Hoffman proclaimed that the remodeling created "The most uniquely beautiful lakeside supper club in America."

In August 1961, Ishnala was part of the largest manhunt in Wisconsin history. It began when three men were drinking at the bar, tipping excessively, and ordering several bottles of champagne that they shared with others. Waitresses noticed them spending large amounts of money from wads of bills "the size of an orange." Two of the men wandered upstairs, which was normally closed to the public, looked into an office, then tried another door, which happened to be Cy's room. Finding it locked, they finally returned to the bar. Their actions prompted a call to the authorities, as an armed robbery earlier that week in Sun Prairie was carried out by three men who made off with $3,000 in cash. Two officers discovered that a black Oldsmobile in the parking lot had a stolen license plate. When the three men left Ishnala and got into the car, the police followed

ISHNALA'S BOB PROSSER

During his five-decade career, including his time working at the Hoffman Houses in the Midwest, current Ishnala owner Bob Prosser got to know five of the Hoffman brothers: Fran, Cy, Cos, and Chuck. Cos used to bring his family to Ishnala for the season-opening every year. Prosser recalls, "Cos was so smooth—all the guys were good-looking and knew how to deal with people, and that made them comfortable. The Hoffmans were ahead of their time—they were a big deal before anybody else, they had such a great reputation. They were just great restauranteurs. The brothers didn't worry about the numbers, they figured if they gave people something at a fair price, everything would fall into place. They were great at assembling good people to work for them. I was proud to work for them, even as a busboy at age sixteen. They had this motto, 'It's not the number of people we serve, it's the number of people we please.' That simple phrase has been stuck in my head. Of course, we want to serve more people—we all do—but not at the expense of customer service."

and eventually pulled them over. As the officers walked towards the car, the men opened fire, killing Sauk County officer James Jantz and seriously wounding Lake Delton Police Chief Eugene (Bob) Kohl. The trio drove off, and a manhunt followed, involving 300 volunteers and two airplanes. All three suspects were eventually caught, found guilty of first-degree murder, and given life sentences in Waupun.

In August of 1966, Mirror Lake State Park was opened to the public after years of debate and controversy over its creation. More than 2,000 acres became available for camping, boating, and other recreation. Having the state park as a neighbor meant that Ishnala remained a remote and peaceful destination compared to the other heavily visited areas of the Wisconsin Dells. In the mid-1970s, controversy over the upkeep of the dam that kept Mirror Lake intact involved the Hoffman brothers as owners of both Ishnala and the dam. A major investment was needed to keep the dam in place; otherwise, it would be demolished, and the lake would disappear. After some wrangling between the state and county, the dam was eventually repaired. To this day, Mirror Lake continues to be the showpiece of the park and the supper club. Photos of all nine of the Hoffman brothers keep watch over the Arrowhead Bar. Additionally, the live trees growing through the roof of the dining room are named for each brother, indicated by a round name tag on the trunk.

Frenchy's

Located on Milwaukee's East Side at the intersection of East North Avenue and Kenilworth Place, Frenchy's featured dining, dancing, and drinks. In its earliest days, it also offered entertainment by national acts like Art Tatum, Louis Armstrong, Bobby Short, and Tommy Sheridan. In 1963, owner Paul "Frenchy" La Pointe razed the original building at 1827 East North Avenue and had a French-style country house built just behind it. It became well known in the 1960s and '70s for its exotic selection of game specialties. Dinners included Frenchy's "famous" *hors d'oeuvres* cart, which was essentially a huge relish tray on wheels. Waitresses wore revealing French maid outfits and prepared Caesar salads, bananas flambé, and crepes suzette table side.

La Pointe's son, Paul Reggie, remembers that "everyone famous in the world of art, politics, business, or sports" dined at Frenchy's, including Green Bay Packers coach Vince Lombardi; Mel Blanc, the man of a thousand voices; and ballet dancer Rudolf Nureyev, among others. Frenchy retired in 1974 and sold the property to business partners William T. Schmitt and George Steele. However, the pair declared bankruptcy less than two years later. Clifford's Supper Club owner Clifford Schill bought Frenchy's, kept

Frenchy's exterior, 1963 PHOTO BY LYLE OBERWISE, COURTESY OF MILWAUKEE COUNTY HISTORICAL SOCIETY

Frenchy's

DELICACIES & GAME SPECIALTIES
IN SEASON

Buffalo Steak
LARGE, JUICY, BUFFALO STEAK. SERVED WITH WILD RICE AND
CURRANT JELLY--------------------------------$6.50

Chopped Buffalo Steak
CHOPPED SIRLOIN OF BUFFALO, PAN BROILED WITH SLICED
ONIONS-------------------------------------$4.20

Bear Steak at Orange
STEAKS OF YOUNG NORTHERN BLACK BEAR,
SERVED WITH WILD RICE AND ORANGE SAUCE---------$6.25

Elk Steak au Chaucer
SAUTEED IN BUTTER AND SERVED WITH WILD RICE AND
CURRANT JELLY------------------------------$7.25

Whole Roasted Quail
PLUMP, TENDER, QUAIL ROASTED WITH SAVORY HERBS. SERVED
WITH RICH SOUR CREAM SAUCE UNDER A BELL WITH WILD
RICE AND SPICED APPLE-----------------------$6.95

Roast Mallard Duck
WHOLE WILD DUCK ROASTED WITH WILD RICE DRESSING AND
SERVED WITH BIGARADE SAUCE------------------$7.25

Venison Steak
SAUTEED CHOICE VENISON STEAK SERVED WITH WILD RICE AND
GUAVA JELLY-------------------------------$6.50

Australian Hare
FROM "THE LAND DOWN UNDER", PLUMP, SUCCULENT RABBIT.
SAUTEED WITH CHICKEN LIVERS IN A DELICIOUS WINE AND
TARRAGON SAUCE----------------------------$6.50

Norwegian Reindeer Steak
SINCE THE DAYS OF LIEF ERICKSON, THESE THICK, JUICY
STEAKS HAVE BEEN A NORDIC FAVORITE. SERVED SAUTEED
WITH HUNTERS SAUCE AND WILD RICE--------------$6.75

Chukkar Partridge
STUFFED WITH FRESH FRUIT, PAN BROWNED WITH SALT PORK
AND THEN GLAZED WITH A RED CURRANT WINE JELLY AND
SERVED WITH WILD RICE----------------------$8.95

Norwegian Ptarmigan
FEATHER FOOTED GROUSE FROM THE FROSTY NORTH THEY ARE
ESPECIALLY DELICIOUS WHEN GRILLED WITH BUTTER AND
SERVED WITH BRANDIED MANDARIN ORANGES---------$8.25

Scotch Grouse
A GOURMET DELIGHT FROM THE LAND OF HEATHER. SERVED
DISJOINTED EN CASSEROLE WITH FRESH MUSHROOMS-----$9.25

Deep South Raccoon
AS TRADITIONAL AS "HOG JOWLS AND HOMINY GRITS", CHOICE
CUTS OF RACCOON ARE SIMMERED IN A RICH CREAM
SAUCE AND SERVED WITH PIPING HOT BAKING POWDER BISCUIT-$6.25

Australian Kangaroo
ANOTHER DELICACY FROM THE "LAND DOWN UNDER", TENDER
JUICY KANGAROO STEAK SERVED SAUTEED IN BUTTER-----$6.75

ABALONE
THE SIRLOIN OF THE SEA
This light, filling, succulent shellfish
from the cold Pacific is sauteed and served piping hot with tangy tartare sauce.
$4.25

Frenchy's exotic
game menu

the name, but changed the concept to Dixieland. It, too, did not do well and closed
soon after. Schill later rented the building to a number of businesses, including 1812
Overture Records & Tapes and a health-food market and diner called Beans & Barley,
which remains there today. A fire destroyed the wooden building in 1993, and a new
steel and brick building was erected. Frenchy, who passed away in 1981 at the age of
seventy-two, might have appreciated the irony of a restaurant for vegetarians taking
the place of his celebrated house of meat.

1946

Come to
MARTY'S SHOWBOAT
AND GOLF COURSE
HIGHWAY 32, 4 MILES EAST
THREE LAKES, WIS.

• ENTERTAINMENT
• GOLF • RIDING
• SWIMMING • FISHING
Don't Miss the Boat!

1942

Marty's
Showboat

Takes Pleasure in Intro-
ducing the Sensational

Boogie Woogie King
Mr. Edward Dudley

Opening the 1942 Summer
Season
Saturday, May 2
Highway 32, 3 Miles East
of Three Lakes, Wis.

Marty's Showboat

Carl Marty was a cheesemaker in Monroe, Wisconsin. He sold the business in 1939 and opened Marty's Showboat with the help of his brother Robert on property their father had purchased in 1915. Situated on the shoreline of Big Stone Lake, which is part of the largest chain of inland lakes in the world, the nautical-themed supper club was known for its remote, Northwoods location, fine food, and entertainment that rivaled that of big city clubs—including an appearance by Gypsy Rose Lee, the famous burlesque stripper. In 1946, the Showboat became part of Marty's luxury resort, The Northernaire. Built for $240,000, it was known as "The Waldorf of the Wilderness," and featured a wide range of recreational activities, including golfing, fishing, swimming, and horseback riding. Carl Marty became known for his affinity for wildlife, and one of the attractions of the resort was seeing woodland animals romping around the grounds. There was a beaver named "Bopper," two otters known as "Sugar and Spice," and a porcupine named "Ouch." A tame deer named Billy was also a popular attraction for visitors who enjoyed posing for pictures with him. Sadly in 1946, he was killed by three hunters from Milwaukee who were later arrested and fined $175. A book titled *Mr. Conservation: Carl Marty and His Forest Orphans* by August Derleth was published in 1971. After Marty died in 1979, the Showboat and the Northernaire were passed between a series of owners; eventually, both were demolished. In 2007, the Northernaire was rebuilt as a condominium resort with one- and two-bedroom apartments, cabins, and villas.

Chapter 7

TAKE ME OUT TO THE BALL GAME

THE 1950s

In the 1950s, the golden age of American capitalism dovetailed with the dawn of the halcyon days of the supper club era. Downtown Milwaukee came alive as people spent money more freely at theaters, department stores, hotels, taverns, restaurants, and nightclubs. Older buildings were demolished to make way for acres of new parking lots to hold the growing number of cars. Steakhouses dominated the dining scene, and each claimed they served the city's biggest cut of beef. However, the real excitement was that Major League Baseball was coming to town. In 1953, the Boston Braves traded Bean Town for Brew City to become the Milwaukee Braves. Thrilled nightclub owners saw potential dollar signs from game-day crowds stopping by for dinner and a show. To ensure a boost to their bottom line, they brought in big-name entertainment. Luckily, there was no shortage of famous names willing to grace the stages of Milwaukee's supper clubs.

Billboards on the corner of Plankington Avenue and Kilbourn Avenue, and City Hall in the background, Milwaukee, 1953

93

Holiday House

For a little over fifteen years, a building on the corner of East Clybourn Avenue and North Van Buren, in what was then part of Milwaukee's Italian Third Ward, was the most significant entertainment supper club in the state. The Holiday House opened in December of 1949 and featured an array of top national celebrity singers and comedians. The location had previously been home to the Miami Club during the 1930s, then the Showboat in the 1940s. Owned by John Volpe and Bruno Ramazini, the Holiday House name was inspired by the 1942 Bing Crosby movie *Holiday Inn*. The menu included hand-drawn images of twenty-one holidays, from New Year's Eve to Christmas, and the interior of the club had several window displays along the walls depicting certain holidays throughout the year, including one honoring the July birthdays of Volpe and Ramazini. The club's radio jingle was heard on Midwestern radio stations: "You can have a holiday, each and every day, at Milwaukee's finest supper club, the Holiday House!" There were two rooms in the club: a piano bar that also served luncheons and the main dining room with a large bar and the stage. Between the two,

Holiday House exterior, circa 1950s PHOTO BY LYLE OBERWISE, COURTESY OF MILWAUKEE COUNTY HISTORICAL SOCIETY

the club accommodated several hundred guests. The menu included a range of dishes such as broiled pompano, deep-fried frog legs, lobster tails with butter, baked ham, chicken cacciatore, spaghetti, steaks, and prime rib. Appetizers, salads, and sandwiches, along with desserts, rounded out the menu, which was served until 1:00 a.m. For dinner, every table featured a lazy Susan with relishes and marinated herring. Schlitz was the beer of choice, possibly because Volpe's brother Dominic was a sales rep for the "Beer that Made Milwaukee Famous."

John Volpe's daughter, Susan Vallet, who owned the Brewster's on Downer restaurant in Milwaukee from 1977 to 1988, recalled, "The food was really good, there were lots of private parties there for weddings and birthdays. Frankie Avalon sang for me and my friends on my sixteenth birthday." Volpe booked acts through a talent agency on Rush Street in Chicago; Wisconsin native Hildegarde Loretta Sell, who performed as simply Hildegarde, was the very first entertainer to play the Holiday House. Another local talent that frequently played there was Liberace, who used to send the Volpe family gifts at Christmas time. Volpe, who was born in 1920 and died at the age of eighty-seven, was a steward at Allis Chalmers during the war and later owned the Italian Village restaurant in the Third Ward and the Ardmore Bar (later Caffrey's) on the Marquette campus before opening the Holiday House. "Lots of doctors and lawyers remembered my father from their Marquette days and they followed him to the Holiday House," recalls Susan.

When the Braves moved to Milwaukee in 1953, Volpe and Ramazini saw the opportunity to attract a post-game crowd by placing an ad in the local papers offering $1,500 in cash for any Braves pitcher that pitched a no-hit, no-run game, $500 for a one-hit, no-run game, and $250 for a two-hit, no-run game. While payoffs like that would be absolutely verboten today, there is no record of a player taking the money; however, that same year, a pair of burglars grabbed some $15,000 in cash when they broke into the Holiday House and stole a safe. It was later found broken and empty on Commerce Street under the Humboldt Avenue bridge. In 1954, after Milwaukee tavern owner John DiTrapani was found shot to death in his Cadillac, not far from the

Holiday House, Volpe began receiving threats over the telephone. One caller called him a "cop lover," and another threatened, "We're going to get you," and demanded money. Volpe began to carry an unloaded .38 automatic, and police stepped up their investigations of DiTrapani and other unsolved Mob-related murders.

The string of bad luck continued in June 1956, when a kitchen fire, caused by an overheated air duct clogged with grease, forced 140 customers to be evacuated while the blaze was extinguished. The damage was estimated at nearly $6,000, and the club closed for almost a month while a new kitchen was installed, along with a second entrance and marquee added to the Van Buren side of the building. That same year, the city of Milwaukee began to move forward with plans to redevelop the Third Ward, which included clearing land for a freeway and light industrial use. Targeted by city planners, the Holiday House's liquor license would only be renewed if Volpe signed a waiver agreeing to surrender the license upon thirty days' notice. Feeling pressured, he signed "under protest," and he, along with other business owners, took their fight to City Hall, which helped delay the project for a while. This allowed Volpe and Ramazini to install a new charcoal steak pit in the main dining room. Customers enjoyed steaks served still sizzling on hot coals.

In the summer of 1959, the Holiday House began booking bigger names by once again hiring "The Incomparable" Hildegarde for a seven-day return engagement, followed by Vic Damone, Johnnie Desmond, Peggy King, and the Vagabonds. Lenny Bruce appeared in the fall of 1960 and bombed during

The St. Louis Cardinals and John Volpe (fourth from right), circa 1950s COURTESY OF TOM VOLPE

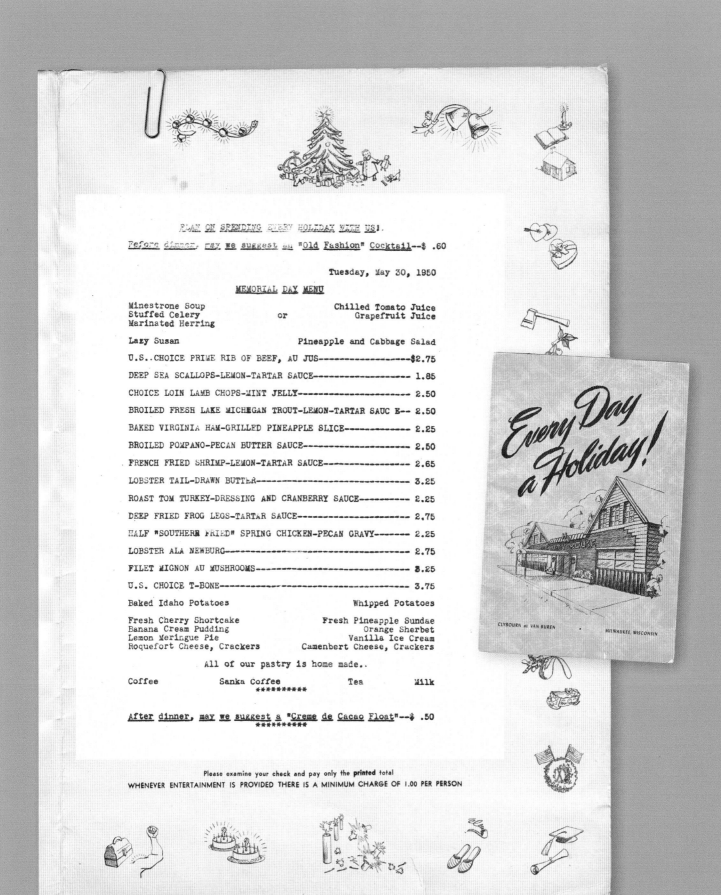

PLAN ON SPENDING EVERY HOLIDAY WITH US!.

Before dinner, may we suggest an "Old Fashion" Cocktail--$ .60

Tuesday, May 30, 1950

MEMORIAL DAY MENU

Minestrone Soup		Chilled Tomato Juice
Stuffed Celery	or	Grapefruit Juice
Marinated Herring		

Lazy Susan   Pineapple and Cabbage Salad

U.S..CHOICE PRIME RIB OF BEEF, AU JUS----------------$2.75

DEEP SEA SCALLOPS-LEMON-TARTAR SAUCE-------------------- 1.85

CHOICE LOIN LAMB CHOPS-MINT JELLY----------------------- 2.50

BROILED FRESH LAKE MICHIGAN TROUT-LEMON-TARTAR SAUCE-- 2.50

BAKED VIRGINIA HAM-GRILLED PINEAPPLE SLICE------------- 2.25

BROILED POMPANO-PECAN BUTTER SAUCE--------------------- 2.50

FRENCH FRIED SHRIMP-LEMON-TARTAR SAUCE----------------- 2.65

LOBSTER TAIL-DRAWN BUTTER------------------------------ 3.25

ROAST TOM TURKEY-DRESSING AND CRANBERRY SAUCE---------- 2.25

DEEP FRIED FROG LEGS-TARTAR SAUCE--------------------- 2.75

HALF "SOUTHERN FRIED" SPRING CHICKEN-PECAN GRAVY------- 2.25

LOBSTER ALA NEWBURG----------------------------------- 2.75

FILET MIGNON AU MUSHROOMS----------------------------- 3.25

U.S. CHOICE T-BONE------------------------------------ 3.75

Baked Idaho Potatoes   Whipped Potatoes

Fresh Cherry Shortcake	Fresh Pineapple Sundae
Banana Cream Pudding	Orange Sherbet
Lemon Meringue Pie	Vanilla Ice Cream
Roquefort Cheese, Crackers	Camenbert Cheese, Crackers

All of our pastry is home made..

| Coffee | Sanka Coffee | Tea | Milk |

****

After dinner, may we suggest a "Creme de Cacao Float"--$ .50
****

Please examine your check and pay only the **printed** total
WHENEVER ENTERTAINMENT IS PROVIDED THERE IS A MINIMUM CHARGE OF 1.00 PER PERSON

Every Day a Holiday!

CLYBOURN at VAN BUREN   MILWAUKEE, WISCONSIN

Holiday House Memorial Day Menu specials, 1950

the 6:30 p.m. dinner show. Volpe, who was a fan of Bruce's comedy, went up to him afterward and said, "Lenny! We had so many walkouts!" Bruce replied, "I'm hip, man. They were stepping on my feet." It was his second strikeout in Milwaukee, and he later incorporated the experience into his act titled "The Gray Line Tour Crowd."

OPENING TONITE!
TONY BENNETT
America's No. 1
TV and Recording Artist
Appearing thru AUG. 13th
including
This SUN., AUG. 7th
SHOW
TIMES:
Dinner Show
8:30 P. M.
Supper Show
10.30 P. M.
and Late Show
12.30 P. M.
SUNDAY
MATINEE
at 5 P. M.
Dinner Show
8 P. M.
Supper Show
10.30 P. M.
DINNERS from $3.00
COVER CHARGE
$2.00 Nightly and $2.50 Saturdays
HOLIDAY HOUSE
Clybourn at Van Buren
BR. 2-4234

1960

In January 1964, Volpe, after deciding that the big-name entertainers were asking for too much money (Tony Bennett was paid $10,000), began offering Gay Nineties entertainment, which was a national trend at the time. Local musician Skip Wagner and his banjo orchestra, dressed in straw boaters and striped blazers, played singalong numbers followed by silent movies starring Charlie Chaplin and Fatty Arbuckle. Waitresses wore flapper outfits and delivered buckets of draft beer along with "The Al Capone," a broiled bratwurst on an Italian roll and "The Big Jim Diamond," a tenderloin steak sandwich. Going in a completely different direction, the smaller "A-Go-Go Room" featured female go-go dancers and the latest dance hits played by WRIT disc jockey Tex Meyer, who broadcasted live while the crowd was on the dance floor doing the Twist, Frug, Gorilla, and Watusi. That same year, the booking of belly dancer Little Egypt broke the Holiday House attendance record during her two-week run, with a total of 13,600 people catching her act. Just prior to the Little Egypt shows, co-owner Bruno Ramazini left the Holiday House and became the new general manager of the Leilani supper club in Brookfield.

On Saturday, June 19, 1965, a full house had enjoyed a performance by the popular Chicago doo-wop group, The Flamingos, and by 3:30 a.m., everyone had left, and the club shut down for the night. Shortly afterward, in the early morning dawn of Father's Day, a fire broke out in a garbage can behind the bar, and a broken gas line helped spread the flames throughout the building. Damage estimates were between $80,000 and $100,000. Volpe, hoping the club would be rebuilt, initially planned to keep his fall entertainment schedule; however, the club never reopened, and he decided to retire. The remains of the building were razed, and the property has been a parking lot ever since. A couple of years later, the boundaries of the Third Ward moved a block south to St. Paul Avenue as the long-planned Lake Freeway extension from I-94/43 was built, causing the destruction of many buildings between Clybourn and St. Paul, including the beloved Blessed Virgin of Pompeii Catholic Church, affectionately known to the parishioners as the "Little Pink Church." (When the freeway extension was built, it stopped just east of Van Buren Street. In 1979, that unfinished bit of elevated highway was used in the John Belushi and Dan Ackroyd comedy, *The Blues Brothers*, during the now-legendary car chase scene where the Ford Pinto full of Illinois Nazis drives off the end of the road.)

(Left to right) John Volpe, Vic Colacino, Bev Colacino, Hazel Volpe,
Dean Martin, 1950s COURTESY OF MICHAEL VOLPE

MILWAUKEE'S FINEST SUPPER CLUB

holiday house

HOLIDAY HOUSE ENTERTAINERS

Frankie Avalon	Gene Krupa
Jim Backus	Julius La Rosa
Tony Bennett	Liberace
Lenny Bruce	Dean Martin
Freddie Cole	Vaughn Monroe
Vic Damone	Wayne Newton and
Johnnie Desmond	Jerry Newton
Phyllis Diller	Patti Page
Little Egypt	Les Paul and Mary Ford
The Flamingos	Johnny Puleo
Hildegarde	Della Reese
Lionel Hampton	Dan Rowan and
Al Jarreau	Dick Martin
The Ahmad Jamal Trio	Sophie Tucker
Louis Jordan	Vagabonds
Peggy King	Andy Williams
George Kirby	Billy Williams

Now Appearing
Thru July 16th
BILLY
WILLIAMS
and
His
Revue

DINNERS
from
$3.00

Dinner Show . . . 8:30 P. M.
Supper Show . . . 11:30 P. M.

HOLIDAY HOUSE
Clybourn at Van Buren
BR. 2-4234

Ray Jackson's

In the early 1950s, sports bars didn't exist as they do today. Corner bars with a small black-and-white TV tuned to a boxing match or baseball game were about all there was. However, there was one supper club in Milwaukee that had a strong connection to sports—Ray Jackson's, on Bluemound Road.

Previous to opening his restaurant, Jackson managed a Russian boxer and later became a ringside judge. In 1950, he decided to open a cocktail lounge on the corner of Muskego Avenue and Mitchell Street on Milwaukee's south side. Business was slow until he began serving hamburgers and sandwiches. In March of 1953, Ray, along with other baseball fans in Wisconsin, was thrilled to hear that the Boston Braves would become the Milwaukee Braves, ending a fifty-two-year absence of big-league play in town. Shortly afterward, Ray decided to open a new restaurant close to County Stadium where the Braves played. In early 1954, he opened Ray Jackson's in the former Tam O'Shanter tavern at 5118 West Bluemound Road. The supper club was decorated with sports memorabilia, and a sign painted on the front door welcomed customers with: "Through these doors pass the world's greatest fans."

Ray Jackson's became an overnight success as the post-game hangout for baseball players and other sports figures. In addition to being ideally situated near the stadium, before the freeway was built, Bluemound Road was the main artery heading west from downtown, and Jackson's was a convenient place for office workers to stop for a martini or two on their way home.

Ray's son Jimmy, co-owner of the Jackson Grill supper club on 38th Street and Mitchell Street, recalls, "My father's place was one of the first sports bars in the United States. There wasn't even a TV in the place, it was just filled with sports personalities constantly. It started off with the [Milwaukee] Braves. It was unbelievable to walk into [Ray Jackson's] as a child; I never wanted to

"Where Good Sports and Good Food Meet"

RAY Jackson's
HOUSE OF HITS

5118 W. Blue Mound Rd.
SPring 1-2300
At the Entrance to the Stadium
AAA Approved

leave. I remember I got a job washing dishes when I was thirteen and I didn't want a day off, I wanted to be around there all the time because of the baseball players. I got to meet everyone in the sports world there: [boxing legends] Joe Louis and James J. Braddock, [Milwaukee Braves player and Brewers' announcer] Bob Uecker, even [baseball legend] Joe DiMaggio. My father collected 1,500 signatures of sports figures, writers, and celebrities, and had many of them up on the walls."

Jackson's was also a favorite of legendary Green Bay Packers coach Vince Lombardi, who always ate lunch there on the Saturdays before NFL games at County Stadium. For their post-game bus ride back to Green Bay, Ray made sandwiches for the team and included a few martinis in cleverly disguised containers for Coach Lombardi. Above the main dining room and bar, there was a second-floor banquet room called the Clubhouse, which seated about sixty people. A variety of groups held meetings in there, including the World Series Club of Milwaukee, organized by Harvey Kuenn, baseball player and later the manager of the Brewers. Jimmy remembers, "A ball player would come in and do a presentation. [The World Series Club] is still going today."

Ray Jackson, 1979

ROSIN BAKED POTATOES

The lost art of cooking potatoes in rosin was practiced at Ray Jackson's. Originally a southern tradition, it calls for a large pot and several pounds of rosin—the solid amber residue left over after the distillation of turpentine. The potatoes cook in the boiling rosin for nearly an hour before they are served. The result is the most delicious baked potato ever, far superior to any other baking method, or so it is said. The skin isn't eaten, however, because it's covered in rosin.

The mainstay of the food at Ray Jackson's was prime rib and steaks served with a rosin baked potato (see sidebar). Ray made all his own salad dressings by experimenting with the day chef, Frankie Rodriguez, who was from New Orleans. Their most popular concoction was called Chef's Secret, which had seventeen herbs and spices. "My father decided to bottle it, so he put an ad in the Sunday *New York Times* and got orders for 600 bottles," Jimmy recalls. "He found it was so much trouble to make, pack, and ship, that he canceled the ad for the next week. After that he only gave out bottles for Christmas."

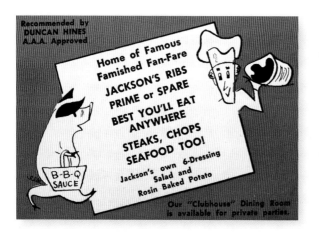

1965 turned out to be an unlucky year for baseball fans in Milwaukee and Ray Jackson. It began with the construction of the I-94 freeway, which cut off the connection from the stadium and Bluemound Road. Then, after twelve years in Milwaukee, the Braves were sold and moved to Atlanta at the end of the season. The most serious misfortune occurred on September 5, when Ray Jackson's went up in flames. Jimmy recalls, "It started with an electrical fire in the kitchen, which did $40,000 in damage. It was devastating because the insurance man was pocketing the payments, so when my father put in a claim, there was no insurance. He found out the agent had scammed other businesses as well, and when he took him to court, the agent died of a massive heart attack. So, he had to start over from scratch with his own money. I was proud of my father for doing that."

After the fire, Ray moved into the building next door. However, he was only permitted to lease two-thirds of it, which didn't leave enough room for a kitchen. Without being able to serve food, Ray turned the place into a discotheque with a glass dance floor lit from the bottom and murals of dancing women. "Go-go clubs were big then, and he jumped on top of it, otherwise he would have nothing," according to Jimmy.

By August 1967, Ray put an end to the go-go dancing—to the great relief of many longtime customers—when he was able to lease the rest of the space and open his kitchen. While Milwaukee was still without a ball club that year, businessman Allan "Bud" Selig managed to get the Chicago White Sox to play an exhibition game against the Minnesota Twins at County Stadium. The game drew a sold-out crowd of over 51,000, and the White Sox returned for ten games during the 1968 season. Selig, who was good friends with Ray, eventually bought the Seattle Pilots in 1970, and they became the Milwaukee Brewers. With baseball back at County Stadium, ballplayers and fans returned to Ray Jackson's. "Customers were pretty good about not pestering them while they were eating," Jimmy said. "After washing dishes, I started bartending and began a twelve-year apprenticeship under Jahn Kramph, who was the night chef at Ray Jackson's. Jahn was from Austria, and we'd make sauerbraten and pepper steak for lunch, but stayed with what we were known for at dinner like steaks and ribs."

Ray Jackson's advertisement, 1971

In 1984, plans to build a 450-inmate prison near County Stadium were opposed by both Selig and Ray Jackson, who sued the state to stop the plans from moving forward. Ultimately, the prison wasn't built, but in September of 1986, Ray and his wife LaVerne decided to retire. "It was a pretty sad thing," said Milwaukee Brewers manager George Bamberger at the time. Ray Jackson's had been his "favorite watering hole" during his years with the Brewers. The location at 5108 West Bluemound Road was subsequently home to a number of restaurants, including Fat Valdy's Bar & Grill De Fiesta Garibaldi, which closed in December 2020.

El Dorado

Originally opened in 1954 by Clarence "Sonny" Sommerfield, a restauranteur who owned Sonny's Sandwich Shops and the Homestead Restaurant on Layton Avenue, El Dorado had formerly been the Swiss Inn. Located on the southwest corner of Highway 100 and Bluemound Road, Sommerfield called it "The Cadillac of Eating Houses." The interior sported a Spanish motif in the Arena Dining Room and Fiesta Cocktail Lounge with wall paintings depicting figurines on horseback, illuminated by blacklight. Live entertainment and dancing were provided nightly. El Dorado featured "Steak out of this world," which included Pizzaro's [sic] Demand, a large T-bone cut; Ponce De Leon's [sic] Treasure, a broiled filet mignon with mushroom sauce; and Cortez Delight [sic], a choice top sirloin steak. Fresh Lake Michigan whitefish, Lake Superior trout, and a variety of seafood were also available, along with *à la carte* sandwiches served with radishes,

celery, and carrot sticks. Dinners began with a "large" lazy Susan. Sommerfield over-saw a $200,000 remodeling and expansion that was unveiled in early 1966 and nearly tripled the size of the dining rooms and bar. After Sommerfield retired in 1972, Joseph Stupar ran El Dorado until it closed; he filed for bankruptcy in 1984. The property later became Edwardo's Natural Pizza, but it closed in 2014. Johnny Vassallo, the owner of Mo's Restaurants, including Mo's Irish Pub located across the street, purchased the property along with two partners in 2016. Plans were announced in August of 2020 to construct a twenty-five-story building with 350 luxury apartments. Despite an initial rejection of the plans by the City of Wauwatosa, Vassallo's development group began demolition of the existing building in December 2020.

Buenos Dias! This is **El Dorado** **Buenos Dias!**

10845 WEST BLUEMOUND ROAD, MILWAUKEE, WIS.   Dial SPring 4-8800

SPECIAL A LA CARTE SANDWICHES

BROILED NEW YORK STRIP SIRLOIN	3.00
BROILED TENDERLOIN—OPEN FACE	1.85
BROILED CHOPPED SIRLOIN—U. S. CHOICE BEEF	1.00
CLUB HOUSE—3 DECKER	1.50
BACON, LETTUCE AND TOMATO—ONE OF OUR BEST	.85
SWISS CHEESE—GENUINE SWISS	.85
AMERICAN CHEESE	.85
BROILED CHEESEBURGER	1.25

(No Club House or Bacon, Lettuce and Tomato Served 5 to 8 P. M.)

SERVED WITH ALL ABOVE:
RADISH ROSE   CELERY STICKS   CARROT STICKS
COLE SLAW AND FRENCH FRIES

A LA CARTE SEA FOOD

FRENCH FRIED SHRIMP PLATE	1.75
JUMBO DEEP SEA SCALLOPS	1.75

INCLUDES:
RELISH   FRENCH FRIES   COLE SLAW

A LA CARTE POTATOES

FRENCH FRIES	.30	HASH BROWN	.35	AMERICAN FRIES	.35
COTTAGE FRIES	.50	LYONNAISE	.35	BAKED POTATO	.30
OUR OWN POTATO PUFFS					.50
FRENCH FRIED ONION RINGS					.60
A LA CARTE MUSHROOM EN CASSEROLE					.75

DESSERTS

CHOCOLATE SUNDAE	.30	SHERBET	.20
CARAMEL SUNDAE	.30	ASSORTED PIES	.30
LIEDERKRANZ CHEESE	.50	CAMEMBERT CHEESE	.50

BEVERAGES

COFFEE	.15	MILK	.15	TEA	.15

"STEAK...OUT OF THIS WORLD"
Gracias Amigo

El Dorado's *à la carte* menu, circa 1960s

John rutten

This is **El Dorado**

This is El Dorado

Buenos Dias!   **Buenos Dias!**

10845 WEST BLUEMOUND ROAD, MILWAUKEE, WIS.   Dial SPring 4-8800

MENU

APPETIZERS

BLUE POINTS ON THE HALF SHELL (In Season)	.90
CRABMEAT ON LETTUCE	.85
CHILLED TOMATO JUICE	.25
JUMBO SHRIMP COCKTAIL SUPREME	.75
MARINATED HERRING IN SOUR CREAM	.60
FRESH LOBSTER MEAT COCKTAIL	.85
OUR OWN FRENCH ONION OR SOUP DU JOUR	.30

Steaks • Chops • Fowl

ELDORADO SUGGESTS

Broiled New York Strip Sirloin
5.25
CORONADO'S   FAVORITE

GARLIC SEASONING AT YOUR REQUEST

BROILED LARGE "T" BONE STEAK (Pizzaro's Demand)	5.50
BROILED FILET MIGNON (Mushroom Sauce PONCE DE LEON'S TREASURE)	4.00
BROILED CHOICE TOP SIRLOIN STEAK (Cortez Delight)	3.75
BROILED CHOPPED SIRLOIN STEAK	2.75
BROILED CENTER CUT PORK CHOPS WITH APPLESAUCE	3.25
BROILED SPRING LAMB CHOPS WITH MINT JELLY	4.00
CHICKEN—COUNTRY STYLE EN CASSEROLE	3.25
ONE-HALF BROILED MILKFED CHICKEN	2.75

DOUBLE PORTERHOUSE OR STRIP SIRLOIN CUT AT YOUR REQUEST (For Two)

(NOT RESPONSIBLE FOR WELL OR EXTRA WELL STEAK)

FRESH SEA FOODS

BROILED AFRICAN LOBSTER TAIL (Drawn Butter)	3.75
STUFFED LOBSTER THERMIDOR WITH TOAST POINTS	4.00
BROILED LAKE SUPERIOR TROUT	3.00
BROILED LAKE MICHIGAN WHITE FISH (Tarter Sauce)	2.75
FRENCH FRIED JUMBO FROG LEGS	3.75
BUTTERFLY FRENCH FRIED SHRIMP	2.75
FRENCH FRIED WHOLE WALL-EYED PIKE (Tartar Sauce)	3.00
BROILED WHOLE WALL-EYED PIKE (Tarter Sauce)	3.25
JUMBO DEEP SEA SCALLOPS (Tarter Sauce)	2.75
COMBINATION SEA FOOD PLATTER (LOBSTER TAIL, FROG LEGS, SHRIMP, SCALLOPS)	3.75

COMPLETE DINNERS INCLUDE:

LARGE LAZY SUSAN . . . CHILLED TOMATO JUICE OR SOUP DU JOUR OR FRENCH ONION . . . GARDEN FRESH TOSSED SALAD WITH CHOICE OF OUR OWN SALAD DRESSING: Roquefort Cheese, French, 1000 Island, Italian, Sour Cream or Vinegar and Oil . . . FRENCH FRIED OR BAKED POTATOES WITH CREAM DRESSING . . . DINNER ROLLS WITH SWEET CREAM BUTTER . . . CHOICE OF BEVERAGE . . . DESSERT

• • •

"EL DORADO STEAKS ARE EXPERTLY SELECTED FROM U. S. CHOICE SCIENTIFICALLY AGED GRAIN-FED STEER BEEF"

"STEAK OUT OF THIS WORLD"

(Souvenir Copies of this Menu, $1.00 each)

GRACIAS AMIGO!

El Dorado's main menu, circa 1960s

The Rainbow Supper Club

Advertised as "The Showplace of the Midwest," the building was originally intended to be a cheese store. It was later modified by owner Dr. H. C. Schmallenberg to house both a supper club and a cheese and gift shop. Located at what was then the intersection of Highways 10 and 45, north of New London (now Highway 54/ Business 45 and North Shawano Street), a twenty-eight-room motel, similarly called the Rainbow, was also part of the property. The supper club had two horseshoe-shaped bars and two dining rooms. Live organ music was featured two nights a week. Complete dinners included roast young Long Island duck, "koshered" corn beef, and buttered new cabbage. A Wednesday night smorgasbord and Sunday brunch were big attractions, as well as dining before and after the Green Bay Packers games. Businessman Russ Gerhard, who bought the Rainbow in 1985, was faced with making major repairs to the aging restaurant in the late 1990s. After giving employees plenty of time to find other jobs, Gerhard sold the property at auction in April of 2000. A branch office of the Wolf River Community Bank opened in 2004, and the Rainbow Motel is still in operation next door.

Green Bay New Year's Eve advertisements, 1963

Always A Featured Entertainer...

into the spotlight will step stars of radio, television, the nightclub circuit and dance band headliners! You will enjoy the talent of these lovelies and they will add a perfect note to your enjoyment of the Supper Club.

DANCING NIGHTLY
EXCEPT SUNDAY

Chapter 8

A YUMMY MUMMY, TURKEY WING-DINGS AND HOT SAKE

THE 1960s

novelty was in vogue in the 1960s. New supper clubs featured quirky architecture and imaginatively decorated interiors. Bartenders mixed unique alcoholic concoctions decorated with little paper umbrellas, while the kids sipped Shirley Temples (7UP with a splash of grenadine, topped with a maraschino cherry) or a Roy Rogers (a splash of grenadine with Coca-Cola). A mix of domestic and imported wines began to show up on menus. Popular choices were Lancers rosé, burgundy from Paul Masson, German Liebfraumilch, and cheap bottles of Italian chianti wrapped in a straw basket. Jazz and rock music began to creep into the clubs, replacing the stale and stuffy old standards. And skin was in—or rather, out in the open, as waitresses were asked to wear revealing costumes and uniforms. It was a reflection of the growing swinging singles lifestyle, promoted by Hugh Hefner's *Playboy* magazine, which had opened up a provocative new Chicago supper club of its own.

Dutch's Sukiyaki House

MILWAUKEE • 1958 TO 1974

A one-of-its-kind dining destination began in the 1940s as a small tavern called Dutch's Airport Bar, located on the northern boundary of Milwaukee's General Mitchell Field (now Mitchell International Airport). When it was expanded into a supper club in 1958 and renamed Dutch's Sukiyaki House, owner Harold "Dutch" Ullmer claimed it was the only authentic Japanese sukiyaki house east of San Francisco. Curious diners eager to try Japanese cuisine in a city full of German, Italian, Polish, and other European favorites began their journey at the Sukiyaki House by crossing a small bridge over a koi pond into the lobby. There they were asked to remove their shoes, as is the custom in Japan. Outfitted in paper slippers, guests were seated at low tables and sat cross-legged on the floor. The namesake dish was prepared in front of them by a Japanese hostess who neatly sautéed sliced beef, shiitake mushrooms, bamboo sprouts, onions, and transparent shirataki noodles in a pan over an electric skillet. Spices and sauces completed the dish, which was topped with a raw egg that

Dutch's Airport Bar, circa 1940s; the Bar after its expansion in 1971 COURTESY OF CHRIS WIKEN

cooked slightly from the heat. The Japanese-born hostesses (many of whom had married ex-GIs from Milwaukee) were dressed in traditional kimono, obi sashes, white socks, and sandals. In addition to a bar, there were two dining areas: the Sukiyaki room with ten paper-screened partitions for dining on Japanese dishes and an upper level that featured booth and counter seating. The menu offered traditional supper club fare, including steaks, walleye, lobster, salad, warm bread, and baked potatoes served with "gobs of butter." Chef Kazko Halbach turned out specialties of teriyaki ribs, chicken, and steak, plus tempura shrimp and vegetables. The novelty of the Japanese dining experience may have initially attracted people to Dutch's, but it was the food that brought them back, as it was often rated one of the top dining destinations in Milwaukee.

You're Afraid to Try **sukiyaki?** ... shame on you! it's great! P.S.: So Are the Cocktails Exotic Atmosphere

DUTCH'S SUKIYAKI HOUSE
900 E. Layton Av. 744-9797 • Open 3 p.m. 7 Days a Week

After an extensive fire in 1971, Dutch remodeled, and the somewhat cramped, low tables were replaced with booths. A couple of years later, an over-zealous thief did some of their own redecorating when they walked off with a nine-foot bamboo tree from the lobby and left a trail of dirt heading out the door.

Dutch was a heavyweight Golden Gloves champion in the 1930s, and in addition to his restaurant business, he was quite an inventor. He held patents on several items, including a heat recovery system for home furnaces. He also opened a drive-in restaurant just east of the Sukiyaki House on Layton Avenue called Go-Burger (the unusually shaped building remains as a hair salon). A line of Dutch's frozen sukiyaki dinners was also developed for retail grocery store sales; Dutch called them a "dish of friendship." In 1968, Dutch and his wife Agnes hosted a seventeen-day escorted tour of Japan, with stops in Tokyo, Kobe, Atami, Beppu, Hiroshima, and Kyoto.

Dutch's souvenir ashtray, sake bottle, and chopsticks

By 1974, Dutch was ready to retire and sold the Sukiyaki House on a land contract to Keith Wiken, who renamed it The Packing House. The new supper club became an equally successful business, known for its steaks, seafood, and very popular fish fry drive-through. While the second-floor dining room is no longer there, some features of Dutch's Sukiyaki House can still be seen in The Packing House, such as the pagoda ceiling, which hangs over the current bar and lounge. Dutch kept busy during his retirement, and his background in pugilism led him to form an organization in 1976 to revive professional boxing at the Eagles Club downtown. Two years later, he and Agnes moved to Las Vegas, where he passed away in 2001 at the age of eighty-nine. Agnes followed seven years later.

Dutch's fan-shaped menu,
circa 1960s COURTESY OF CHRIS WIKEN

Harold "Dutch" Ullmer pouring a potent Golden Dragon cocktail

Tee-Pee Supper Club
TOMAH, 1960 TO 2014

The Tee-Pee Supper Club was opened on the corner of Superior Avenue and East La Crosse Street in February 1960 by the Arcade Tavern and Bowling Association, headed by President Carl Honel, Vice President Colonel Donald "Speed" Schueler, and Secretary-treasurer Donald Kline. The building was originally a livery stable in 1890 and was converted into the Tomah Theatre in the early 1900s. By the late 1950s, it was the site of a restaurant called The Coffee Shop, owned by William and Wanda Springer.

The Tee-Pee was decorated in a "relaxing Indian motif," which extended to the outfits worn by waitresses and the souvenir headdresses that were given to guests. Food was prepared over an open hearth in the dining room. Besides charcoal broiled steaks, the Tee-Pee was known for its extensive salad bar and a $1.50 lunch "special-of-the-day" for the downtown office crowd. In 1964, the Arcade Tavern and Bowling Association purchased the building next door to expand the kitchen and add a 120-seat dining room.

TEE-PEE
SUPPER CLUB
TOMAH, WISCONSIN

Tee-Pee dining room and bar, circa 1960s

The Tee-Pee
Supper Club
in 2012

In the late 1960s, manager Francis Kelly teamed up with silent partner Donald Schueler to purchase the Tee-Pee from the other members of the Arcade Association. Kelly was often seen behind the bar pouring drinks and entertaining customers. His signature greeting when they came in was a loud, "Hello, tiger!" However, Kelly's sunny disposition was about to get dark and stormy. In 1972, state investigators charged him with eight counts of watering down liquor. Kelly claimed he was simply pre-mixing drinks and was eventually cleared when a judge found no intent to defraud. In 1973, he was charged with nine counts of commercial gambling and pled guilty to one count of taking bets during the professional football season. He received a suspended sentence and lost his liquor license for seven days in the fall of 1974. Four years later, Kelly was arrested for selling $4,500 worth of amphetamines and cocaine to an undercover officer over a two-month period. He was sentenced to ten years in the Waupun Correctional Institution in October of 1979. He was sixty-three years old. While Kelly was in the midst of his troubles, he sold the Tee-Pee to Dale Klitzke in the summer of 1975. Klitzke, who was also managing the Burnstead's grocery store in Tomah at the time, recalls Kelly's personality, "He was a character. Everyone loved him. Even though they knew he was dealing drugs, even though he was crazy. He had that kind of personality that people would stop in there just to see him, you know?" Klitzke ran the Tee-Pee until September 1982, when he sold it to David Greenwood. Not long after buying the Tee-Pee, Greenwood opened a café nearby and spent a lot of time and money on it. Eventually, he lost interest in running the Tee-Pee. It went into bankruptcy and was closed, according to Dale Klitzke, for at least a year, possibly two.

A whole new era began in 1990, when Elroy Tavern owner Allan "Ed" Thompson, who, as he put it, was the "younger, smarter" brother of then Wisconsin Governor, Tommy Thompson, purchased the Tee-Pee. In late 1991, he sold it on a land contract, but the new owner lasted only a month. Thompson, who had money troubles of his own, leased it to another restauranteur in 1992, and when that didn't work out, it seemed that the Tee-Pee was closed for good.

In 1993, Thompson, with the help of his sister Juliann, and a sympathetic banker from the Bank of Necedah named Duane Weed, was able to get a loan to repay his debts and reopen the supper club; he renamed it Ed Thompson's Tee-Pee. This time, things fell into place and it wasn't long before he had enough money to buy other buildings on the block so he could expand. The new space had room for a beer garden, a large banquet room, and a video game center. Mr. Ed's Tee-Pee, as it was known, was the town gathering place once again. On Fridays, over 400 fish frys were served, and Thompson began a tradition of hosting a free Thanksgiving dinner for the community every year.

1966

Just when things were going so well, Monroe County investigators raided the Tee-Pee in 1997 and confiscated the club's video gambling machines after witnessing payouts to customers. Thompson was irate and complained that the agents took all the money out of the cash registers. "I suppose people will be able to sleep safer now that my nickel poker machines are gone," said Thompson at the time. When asked if his brother knew about the raid, he said, "Which brother, Artie?" referring to the one brother who wasn't the current governor. Ed claimed he wasn't able to make enough money without the gaming machines, and he became a very vocal proponent of allowing gambling in taverns. This led him to make a bid for mayor of Tomah in 2000. He won and was reelected in 2008. He also ran for governor of Wisconsin as a Libertarian in 2002 but lost to Democrat Jim Doyle. In 2010, he entered the race for state senator in the Thirty-first District as a Republican but lost to Democrat Kathleen Vinehout. During the campaign, Thompson was diagnosed with pancreatic cancer. He died in October 2011 at the age of sixty-six.

After Thompson's death, his sister Juliann took over the Tee-Pee Supper Club, but the business failed and closed in 2014. The building sat empty until January 2016, when it was razed to make way for a proposed $11 million mixed-use development. A newly constructed building opened in early 2019. A restaurant named Murray's on Main now occupies the original site of Tee-Pee Supper Club. It is owned by the mayor of Tomah, Mike Murray. One of the original Tee-Pee neon signs is displayed inside the restaurant, which is now referred to as the Tee-Pee Building.

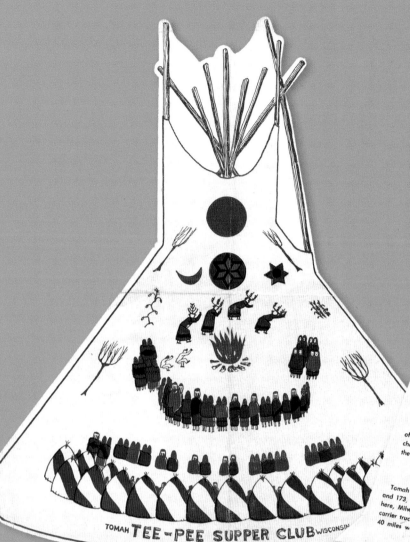

TOMAH **TEE-PEE SUPPER CLUB** WISCONSIN

Tee-Pee Supper Club menu, circa 1960s

AN INDIAN PRAYER

"I come before you, one of your children. I am small and weak; I need your wisdom."

"Let me walk in beauty and make my eyes ever behold the red and purple sunset. Make my hands respect the things you have made; my ears sharp to hear your voice. Make me wise so that I may know the things you have hidden in every leaf and rock."

"I seek strength, not to be superior to my brothers, but to be able to fight my greatest enemy — myself. Make me ever ready to come to you with clean hands and straight eyes, so when life fades as a fading sunset, my spirit may come to you without shame."

———

"THE TEE-PEE SUPER CLUB in downtown Tomah, Wis., offers a relaxing atmosphere in an Indian motif — charcoal broiled food prepared over an open hearth in the dining room. A delightful place to dine."

———

Tomah is located on U.S. 12 and 16, State Highways 21, 131 and 173, Interstate Highways 90 and 94 (Freeway) will divide here, Milwaukee Road and North Western Railways, common carrier truck lines, local airport, Mississippi River transportation 40 miles west.

DINNER MENU

SERVING
DINNERS
5 P.M. - 11 P.M.
SEVEN DAYS A WEEK

NEW YORK STRIP SIRLOIN STEAK -- 4.50
THICK FILLET TENDERLOIN STEAK -- 3.95
LARGE TOP SIRLOIN STEAK ------
CHEF SPECIAL TOP SIRLOIN STEAK - 4.50
LARGE T-BONE STEAK ------------ 3.00
SIRLOIN EN-BROCHETTE ---------- 5.00
CHOPPED SIRLOIN ALA MIGNON ---- 2.75
TENDER CENTER CUT HAM STEAK --- 2.50
TWO CENTER CUT PORK CHOPS ----- 2.50
CHARCOAL BROILED BAR-B Q RIBS - 3.25

COMPLETE DINNERS INCLUDE
Salad and Relish Bar — Soup or Juice
Choice of Baked Potato, French Fries,
Au Gratin, Potato Puff or Hash Browns
Bread Basket — Coffee, Tea or Milk
Dessert

COCKTAILS
MANHATTAN -- 75c
MARTINI ---- 75c
VODKA MARTINI ---- 75c
GIBSON ---- 75c
BEEFEATERS HOUSE OF LORDS 90c
ROB ROY ---- 90c
GIMLET ---- 90c
DAIQUIRI ---- 75c
BACARDI ---- 75c
OLD FASHION ---- 75c
WHISKEY SOUR ---- 75c
MARGARITA ---- 75c
ALL COLLIN'S ---- 75c

SATURDAY SPECIAL
U.S. CHOICE PRIME RIB OF BEEF --- 3.25

LAKE and OCEAN CATCHES
SOUTH AFRICAN LOBSTER, 2-Tails -- 3.25
COMBINATION SEA FOOD PLATE ---- 3.25
PAN FRIED RAINBOW TROUT ------
JUMBO SHRIMP, EN-Brochette ---- 3.25
BATTER FRIED SHRIMP ---------- 2.50
WALL-EYED PIKE -------------- 2.50
SWORDFISH STEAK ------------- 2.50
BREADED SCALLOPS ------------ 2.50
DEEP-FRIED JUMBO FROG LEGS --- 2.50
BREADED SELECT OYSTERS ------- 2.75

NOON
LUNCHEONS
SERVING BEGINNING
AT 11:30 A.M.

A LA CARTE
BEEF TENDERLOIN STEAK SANDWICH 2.50
SPECIAL SIRLOIN STEAK SANDWICH 2.25
¼ FRIED CHICKEN SANDWICH ---- 1.50
CHOPPED SIRLOIN SANDWICH ---- .75
BAKED HAM SANDWICH ---------- .75
BACON, LETTUCE and TOMATO ---- .75
CORNED BEEF ---------------- .75

SALADS
TEE-PEE SALAD 1.25
SHRIMP SALAD ---- 1.35
CHICKEN SALAD ---- 1.35
TUNA SALAD ---- 1.35
COTTAGE CHEESE - FRUIT - 1.25

SANDWICHES
TEE-PEE SPECIAL SANDWICH ---- .80
CORNED BEEF on Hard or Soft Roll - .60
BAKED HAM on Bread, Hard or Soft Roll .60
CHOPPED SIRLON on Hard or Soft Roll .50

NOON LUNCHEON PLATES
GRILLED CHOPPED SIRLOIN STEAK
BREADED VEAL STEAK ----------
CHUCK WAGON STEAK ----------

The printing on the other side is the copy of the work of an Apache chief named Naiche, second in command to the great Geronimo. Done in vegetable dye on doeskin, using a soft buffalo bone for a brush, it pictures the sacred girls' puberty ceremony. While the rest of the tribe watch from in front of their tepees, which face east towards the rising sun, the dance is performed around the purifying fire. Each pair wrapped in a blanket comprises a young girl and an old woman who will act as her guardian. Fertility is symbolized by leafy trees, corn, and wheat; barrenness by leafless trees. The small figures, called Earth Spirits, at the left of the fire, and the posturing Mountain Spirits with candelabra-like headdresses complete the group.

T & C SHOPPER, TOMAH, WISCONSIN

The Pyramid Supper Club

BEAVER DAM • 1961 TO 2009

A pyramid is probably the last thing someone would expect to find in the middle of a Midwestern cornfield. And yet, for nearly fifty years, a pyramid in Dodge County was home to a good, old-fashioned supper club. Located on State Highway 33, between Horicon and Beaver Dam, The Pyramid Supper Club was opened in 1961 by Richard "Dick" and Virginia "Gini" Beth and John and Marie Glavich. Little is known about the Glaviches other than that they were silent partners until 1965. However, the Beths had a rich history in the restaurant business. In 1949, they operated Beth's Bar in Columbus, which sold fish frys for fifty cents. In 1953, they bought the Club 400 just outside of Beaver Dam, which featured $1.75 chicken dinners. By 1957 they were the proprietors of the Maple Lanes Bowling Alley.

It's not clear where the idea to build a pyramid came from, as the Beths had apparently never traveled to Egypt. However, in November 1961, the "Tutankhamun Treasures" exhibition opened at the National Gallery of Art. It traveled to eighteen US cities over the next three years. It is possible that the news of the exhibit inspired their decision.

Postcard
from the
1960s;
opposite:
the dining
room

Construction of the four-story pyramid included a three-bedroom apartment on the second floor for Dick and Gini. Earle Ferguson designed the Egyptian theme in the interior, and Adolph Theiele made relief sculptures of Egyptian figures. Gini later claimed that the Egyptian motif was chosen because of its visual appeal and that there was no intention to associate it with a particular culture's food. She also believed that the pyramid kept her youthful.

The main dining room was called the King Tut Room, which featured a replica of the mummy and artifacts from his tomb. The Nile Room was on the lower level, and on its walls were two murals, a shoreline view of the River Nile and the Cheops pyramid. The Egyptian theme didn't extend to the menu, however; it offered standard American supper club fare. Years later, one Madison restaurant critic wrote that she traveled to the Pyramid to try their Egyptian food and was upset that they didn't have any. Dinners included a lazy Susan (at the Pyramid, it was called a Super Susan) loaded with vegetables and garlic cheese dip, plus soup or juice, fresh shrimp cocktail or herring, mixed green salad, and choice of potato. A couple of specialty cocktails, the Pyramid Surprise and after-dinner Yummy Mummy, playfully resumed the motif. A small gift shop located in the reception area sold Egyptian jewelry.

The Beths employed a staff of forty-five local citizens and were actively involved with the Dodge County Fair. Dick usually placed the winning bid on 4-H beef, pork, and lamb. One year, two friends of the Beths, who were transporting steers from the 4-H sale to the market, instead herded them through the dining room of the Pyramid and became local legends in the process.

Pyramid shaped menu, 1962

THE PYRAMID

The Management

Of our SUPER SUSAN, you may help yourself avail

Next your individual HERRING or SHRIMP COCKTAIL

Then our SOUP OF THE DAY or JUICE it's up to you

Now enjoy your SALAD, VEGTABLE, POTATO you have your choice of TWO

DESSERT, MENTHE or CREME DE-COKE it's delightful of the PYRAMID

Now enjoy your favorite ENTREE, we know you'll say you did

Pyramid Originals

BLACK LILY
A Smooth Combination of Gin and Lime, Flavored with a Berry Liqueur

PYRAMID PUNCH
A Surprise You'll Prize

YUMMY MUMMY
A Tangy After Dinner Refresher

Let's have a Cocktail

ALEXANDER
COLLINS
BACARDI
DAIQUIRI
MARTINI
MANHATTAN
WHISKEY SOUR
OLD FASHIONED
PINK LADY
SINGAPORE SLING
CHAMPAGNE COCKTAIL

SIDE CAR
LONDON FOG
STINGER
B AND B
DRAMBUIE
CHARTREUSE
GRAND MARNIER
CHERRY HEERING
GRASSHOPPER
BLUE TAIL FLY
PINK SQUIRREL

PYRAMID APPETIZER COCKTAILS

Sardines	.60
Crabmeat	.75
Shrimp (for 2)	.50
Antipasto (for 2)	.90
Stuffed Hearts Celery	1.00
Lobster Cocktail	

BEAVER DAM WISCONSIN

PYRAMID SUPREME
SIRLOIN
at its best
4.15

CHOICE	CHOICE
T-BONE STEAK Fit for a Shiek **4.75**	**NEW YORK STRIP STEAK** King Tut's Choice **4.65**

TENDERLOIN STEAK SPECIAL
Tender as Cleopatra's heart
2.95

SPEAR-A-MID SPECIAL
TENDER PIECES OF TENDERLOIN MUSHROOM CAPS — TOMATO GREEN PEPPER PREPARED ON A SKEWER
3.35

FILLET MIGNON
(Large Tenderloin Bacon Wrapped)
Would make a sphinx smile
3.95

Lean CENTER-CUT PORK CHOPS with Apple Sauce
A favorite in Egypt
2.95

Barbecued LOIN RIBS
Served With Tangy Sauce
3.35

DOUBLE SIRLOIN FOR TWO with Fried Onion Rings
7.95

LAMB CHOPS
Mint Jelly
3.95
Never saw the desert

Entrees Ala Carte 50¢ Less

Let Us Help You Plan Your Wedding, Anniversary or Birthday Party

Chopped Sirloin Steak
Nice 'n juicy
2.50

NOT RESPONSIBLE FOR APPEARANCE OR TENDERNESS OF STEAKS ORDERED WELL DONE

We Cater To Group Noon Luncheons By Reservations

PHONE: 885-6611   BEAVER DAM, WIS.

July 1962

LOBSTER TAIL
South African
Broiled to a Pharoah's taste
3.95

SHRIMP
Jumbo Louisiana (Deep Fried) Served with Tartar or Hot Sauce
2.60

CRAB LEGS
ALASKAN KING
Lemon Wedges and Butter
3.95

SCALLOPS
Deep-Sea
2.60

FROG LEGS
Delicious
3.95

Fisherman's Platter
Lobster Pike Shrimp, Scallops, Oysters Assorted Sauces
3.60

DUCKLING
Roast LONG ISLAND with Sage dressing
A real treat
3.50

CURRIE!
How about a . . .

SHRIMP	2.85
LOBSTER	4.00
CHICKEN	2.70

Or perhaps a . . .

NEWBURG!

SHRIMP	2.85
LOBSTER	4.00
CHICKEN	2.70

Are You Lika! Deep Dried . . .

CHICKEN
Milk-Fed
Pan Fried — or Broiled
ONE-HALF
2.50

ROCKY-MOUNTAIN BROOK TROUT
2.85

CANADIAN WALLEYED PIKE
2.60

Pyramid SPECIALS
includes CHOICE OF POTATO AND SALAD HOME-MADE BREAD AND BUTTER AND BEVERAGE

Spring Chicken
Deep Fried
A real winner
1.50

Club Steak
South African Broiled to your taste
2.90

choice Sirloin Steak
Smothered in onions
1.75

Lobster
South African
1.95

Pork Chops
BROILED Lean
1.75

Peppered Lobster
with eggs
2.95

Walleyed Pike
Deep Fried
1.75

Jumbo Shrimp
(Deep Fried) with sauce or hot sauce
1.75

SANDWICHES
(not served during dinner hours)

CHOPPED SIRLOIN	.60
CLUB HOUSE	1.25
LIVER SAUSAGE	.50
WHITE MEAT CHICKEN	.75
BACON, LETTUCE AND TOMATO	

TENDERLOIN TIPS
sauté á with mushrooms
COMPLETE DINNER
3.35

Tenderloin Steak
2.45

ALA CARTE

Saute — Mushrooms	.75
French Fried Onion Rings	.65
Soup — Cup .25	Bowl .35
Potato	.15
Vegetable	.35
Salad	.25
Coffee	.15
Tea	.15
Milk	.15

WE FEATURE
PRIME RIBS OF BEEF
au jus
COMPLETE DINNER **3.25**
EVERY MONDAY — WEDNESDAY — SATURDAY and SUNDAY after 4:30 p.m.
KING SIZE

After nearly forty years in the restaurant business, Dick suffered a stroke in 1986. He died in December 1992 at the age of seventy. Some months later, Gini placed an ad in the local paper:

> *Due to the rumor,*
> *the Pyramid is*
> *Not Closing*
> *and will remain in*
> *business forever with*
> *fabulous food and*
> *service by the great*
> *staff of employees.*
> *—Gini Beth*

While the Pyramid did not close, Gini *did* end up selling it to Pat McGinty a year later. McGinty continued serving the same food and service that the Beths had offered. In September 2000, the Pyramid was sold to Al and Kalen Neumann, who changed the name to the Nile Club. Raymond and Denise Olson purchased it in August of 2006 and renamed it the Pyramid of the Nile. Ray had been in the restaurant business on and off for almost thirty years, and they hoped to use one of the dining rooms to host their newly started Harbor Missionary Church. Things did not work out, however, and the Pyramid of the Nile closed in 2009. The building has been on and off the market since 2010.

A Pyramid Supper Club postcard, 1962 COURTESY OF PAULETTE HORN

THE WAY I SEW IT

One of the Pyramid Supper Club's longtime employees was Nez Miescke. Her daughter Paulette Horn remembers, "My mother worked at the Pyramid from its early days, first as a waitress and later a bartender and hostess. I also worked there briefly in the late '70s as a coat check girl. [The photos] are some of the uniforms my mom wore through the years. Hemlines were going up, as were the hairdos, during this period in history, and these uniforms tell the tale!

"My mom helped design and sew several of the uniforms for herself and other waitresses. I particularly remember the unique fitted number with the pleated skirt and shoulder scarf. She had to order several bolts of white polyester double-knit and yards upon yards of teal and gold ribbon trim. We had quite the flurry of activity at our house for several weeks that year. Waitresses came and went through her sewing room door to be measured and fitted. It was all quite entertaining!"

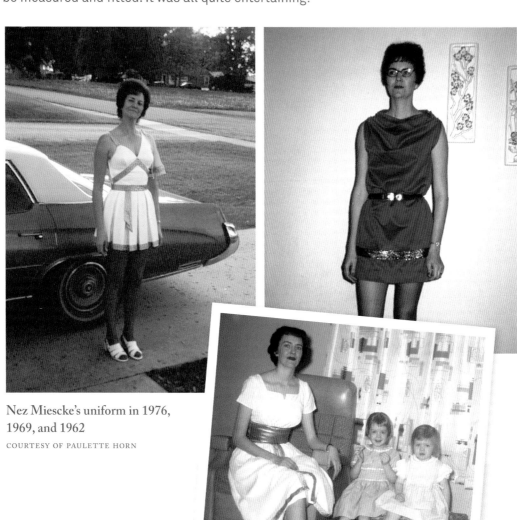

Nez Miescke's uniform in 1976,
1969, and 1962

COURTESY OF PAULETTE HORN

Hartwig's Gobbler Supper Club and Motel

In 1968, forty-nine-year-old turkey farmer Clarence Hartwig decided to sell his poultry direct to customers and opened the Cackle Shack, a supper club that served fried chicken, fish, and prime rib. Located near his processing plant on Highway 26 and I-94 in Johnson Creek, the Cackle Shack was open six days a week and offered dining and dancing on the weekends. On Sundays, family-style turkey dinners were served from noon to 4:00 p.m.

The venture proved to be a big hit, but Hartwig had plans to open something bigger and better. He hired local architect Helmut Ajango to design a new restaurant to be built next to the Cackle Shack. Hartwig admired the innovative direction of Ajango's design of the Fireside Dinner Theatre in Fort Atkinson, but he wanted something even more impressive. The result was a 16,000-square-foot, round building

Above:
Exterior of
Hartwig's
Gobbler
Supper Club
COURTESY OF
JAMES LILEKS

with a white dome, black stone walls, and dark windows shaped to resemble turkey eyes. The entryway walls were covered in petrified wood from New Mexico, and purple shag carpeting was laid throughout. The centerpiece of the interior was a rotating bar, and an elevated dance floor called the Roost. The project cost $1 million, and Hartwig's Gobbler Supper Club opened to the public with great fanfare in May 1969. The main feature of the menu was turkey, along with the usual supper club standards of steak, seafood, and chops. In addition to lunch and dinner, the Gobbler was unique among supper clubs in that it also served breakfast seven days a week.

In late summer of 1971, the equally lavish forty-nine-room Gobbler Motel opened with amenities such as sunken baths, water beds, stereo systems with 8-track tape decks, an indoor pool, and bridal suites. Hartwig booked live acts for both the Gobbler and Cackle Shack and proclaimed that between the two clubs, Johnson Creek was becoming the center of entertainment in Wisconsin. While Frank Sinatra Jr. did perform for five nights during the Gobbler's Las Vegas week, Las Vegas it was not. An attempt to have female bartenders wear sexy outfits backfired after two women were fired for refusing to wear the revealing costumes of black

Interior of
Hartwig's
Gobbler
Supper Club
COURTESY OF
JAMES LILEKS

briefs, fishnet stockings, and open V-neck jackets. The state's Department of Industry, Labor, and Human Relations found the Gobbler guilty of sex discrimination; only male bartenders were hired in the future.

Still, the Gobbler Supper Club and Motel was the most swinging place in Jefferson County. In early 1973, the Cackle Shack closed, and the building and its contents were auctioned off. In the mid-1970s, Clarence Hartwig moved to Sarasota, Florida. He died in Rochester, Minnesota, after suffering a heart attack in 1979. His son Clyde continued to run the Gobbler.

On December 30, 1980, Clyde's brother William stole a semi-trailer truck full of turkey meat from the Hartwig processing plant. He left behind a note in which he demanded money, food, liquor, cigarettes, and a car, and claimed there was a bomb in the factory. No explosives were found, and the truck was later recovered in Chicago. William was charged with extortion, making a bomb threat, burglary, and theft. He was declared unfit to stand trial and committed to the Mendota Mental Health Institute in Madison.

By the late 1980s, the Gobbler was seen as a relic of the past. In July 1992, Clyde closed the supper club and motel, laying off fifty-one employees in the process. The property was eventually sold, and over the years, it became a series of restaurants, including Redondos Mexican and John-John's Ribs. In 1996, attorney Ray Krek and auto dealers Marvin Havill and Daryl Spoerl bought the property for nearly $500,000. They reopened the supper club as The New Gobbler after "giving the old bird a facelift," as Krek put it, to the tune of $600,000 in renovations. However, The New Gobbler lasted less than two years, and closed in 1999. The motel had been reopened as King Arthur's Inn, but it, too, lasted only a couple of years. It sat vacant until 2001 when it was demolished. Plans for a multi-million-dollar casino, hotel, and convention center to be built on the Gobbler property were proposed by the Lac du Flambeau band of the Lake Superior Chippewa Indians but they never materialized. A new venture called the Round Stone Restaurant and Lounge opened in 2002 but didn't last. A proposal in 2003 to turn the property into "Gobbler A-Go-Go," featuring dancers in bikinis and waitresses dressed in Playboy bunny outfits, was unanimously shot down by the Johnson Creek Plan Commission. By 2009, the site was put up for auction, but there were no buyers.

In 2015, new owner Daniel Manesis opened the Gobbler Theater after a $2.7 million renovation. It features live concerts but no food, as the stage replaced the kitchen area. For years after its demise, the Gobbler has been worshipped and mourned by various online blogs. As Dave Hoekstra points out in *The Supper Club Book*, "The Gobbler is larger than life now that it is dead."

Cackle Shack advertisement, 1969; Gobbler advertisement and swizzle stick, 1971

GOBBLER TURKEY PARADE

The Gobbler was all about turkey, so it's no surprise that there were at least twenty turkey dishes on the menu, including:

- Fresh Baked Turkey (white and dark meat in country-style gravy)
- Fresh Baked Turkey (all white meat or all dark meat)
- Country Style Chopped Turkey (deep-fried, all you can eat)
- Country Style Sautéed Turkey Livers
- Entrees include: Lazy Susan, soup or juice, salad, turkey dressing, cranberries, fresh homemade bread, butter, and beverage.

Sandwiches and Coffee Shop Specials:
- Gobbler Turkeyburger
- Gobbler Cheese Turkeyburger
- Gobbler Turkey Reuben Sandwich
- Cold Turkey Sandwich
- Turkey Club Sandwich
- Hot Turkey Sandwich
- Turkey a la King
- Turkey Wing-Ding Luncheon
- Turkey Tom-Tom Luncheon
- Gobbler Salad
- Hartwig's Gobbler Daily

The Red Garter Gals
advertisement, 1971

Welch's Embers

In 1945, Leo Welch purchased The Rosebud Inn, located at 3520 East Washington Avenue, from Jack Kramer and renamed it the Ace of Clubs. Unfortunately, the building was destroyed by a fire on Good Friday in 1958. Welch originally planned to rebuild and keep the Ace of Clubs name, but after some thought, he decided Welch's Embers was more appropriate. It opened in 1960. Boasting a total of six dining rooms, three bars, and capacity for 600 people, it was one of the largest supper clubs in the state. Welch designed the Embers based on feedback he received from questionnaires filled in by patrons of the Ace of Clubs. According to Welch, "A city the size of Madison needed a restaurant with banquet room space sufficient for 250 or more persons, plus adequate room for meetings and receptions. Also needed was a sufficiently large dance floor with bar space. Plus, of course, a kitchen large enough to meet all the catering needs." A staff of ninety-two kept the club running for nearly ten years. In 1969, Welch's Embers was sold to Anthony Q. Sanna and became Maxine's French Quarters and Proud Mary Bistro. The businesses did not do well, and Sanna closed them in April of 1972. The property was then home to a couple of rock clubs called Fat Fanny's and The Spectrum. The building and its contents were sold at auction in July of 1975. In 1978, the building housed a waterbed store, and in 1987, it became Prime Quarter Steak House, the first of a chain of grill-your-own-steak restaurants in Wisconsin. It closed after a fire in May of 2015, and the property is now a gas station and car wash.

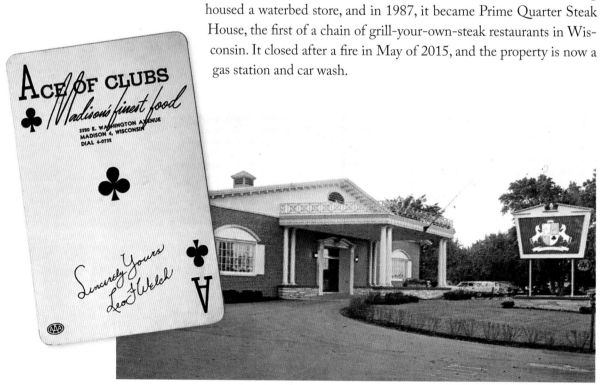

Guzman's Black Hawk Supper Club

The Black Hawk Supper Club was owned by Larry and Virginia Guzman and was located five miles northeast of downtown Janesville on Highway 14. The couple was originally from Chicago; they moved to Janesville in the late 1940s because they wanted to raise their children in a smaller city. They operated the Dutch Mill Candy Shop and a couple of restaurants, including a drive-in on Highway 51 and Larry's at 37 South Main Street, before purchasing the Colonial Acres Restaurant from owner Claire Chapin in August of 1962. With two dining rooms and a cocktail lounge, the restaurant seated 170. Two years later, the name was changed to Guzman's Black Hawk Supper Club, and live music and dancing were featured on weekends. Fillet of haddock was served family-style on Friday nights, along with potato pancakes, cabbage salad, French fries, and rolls and butter for $1.25. The Black Hawk also served businessmen's lunches, and on Sundays, dinner included a selection of prime rib, roast turkey, baked ham, and fried chicken. In December of 1964, a kitchen fire broke out in the Black Hawk and caused extensive damage. Repairs were made, and the Guzmans continued to operate the Black Hawk until they retired and moved to Florida in 1973.

Chapter 9

ARE WE THERE YET?

A car full of hungry people driving in a remote location needed more than confusing verbal directions or a cumbersome and outdated map to locate a supper club. "Are we there yet?" became a familiar refrain, most likely since the days of the Model T. Since then, road signs advertising every-thing from tobacco to Burma Shave have also been a part of the travel landscape. However, the most useful signs combined advertising and information to clearly announce, *Here we are.*

Road Signs

Before GPS technology was introduced in cars and on mobile phones, drivers relied on the help of a well-placed, hand-painted sign along country highways and backroads to guide the way to their destination. Here are a few particularly helpful supper club signs, some of which can still be seen today.

RIVIERA SUPPER CLUB
THOMAS H. LANTZAS, MGR
PHONE HOWARD 324   GREEN BAY, WIS.

Outstanding FACILITIES FOR
• PRIVATE PARTIES
• BANQUETS
• SALES MEETINGS

625 East Detroit Street
Milwaukee • Wisconsin

BR. 2-0886

Located 3 blocks south of
WISCONSIN AVENUE

the Antlers
Supper Club

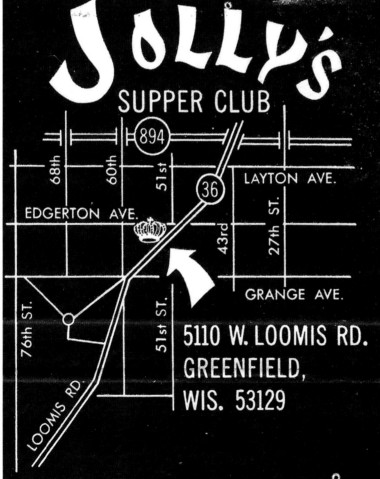

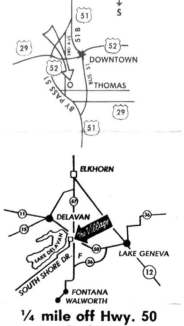

¼ mile off Hwy. 50
on South Shore Drive
on Delavan Lake

Matchbook Maps

During the days when so many people smoked, matchbooks were a great way to advertise and give directions at the same time. Some were perfectly clear, others—not so much.

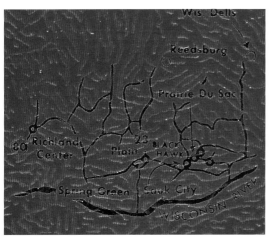

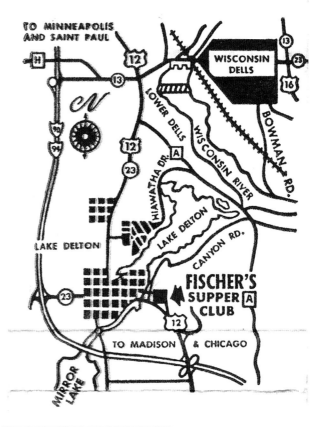

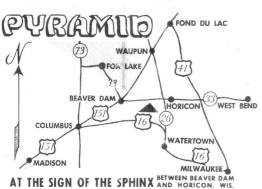

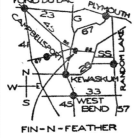

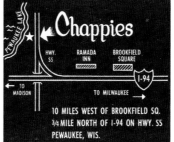

Modern 41
motel
TV Air Conditioned

WELCO E
NIGHLY
AND
WEEKLY

SUNRISE
Motel

VACANCY

PHONE HBO
LOW RATES
CABLE
WIFI

American
MOTEL

Chapter 10

HIGHWAY 41, THE CHICAGO ROAD

In October of 1967, I-94 construction bypassed the old Highway 41 north of the Milwaukee county line, effectively cutting off the motels and supper clubs that depended on the traffic. Suburban expansion has since eliminated most of the vintage buildings on what was known as the Chicago Road; however, some of the mid-century era motels still operate today.

For several decades, US 41 was the main highway that led to Milwaukee. It started as a dirt road in 1922 and was gradually widened and upgraded over the years until eventually, it became Interstate 94. From the very beginning, roadhouses, gas stations, and motels sprung up along the seemingly endless miles of farmland. As highway traffic increased, these pastoral crossroads in Kenosha and Racine counties were quickly transformed into sprawling exits, bustling with activity, where travelers were able to rest, eat, drink, sleep, and shop. Of the many former US 41 roadhouses and supper clubs, three stand out: The Rafters and Ray Bussler's, both in Oak Creek, and Kilbourn Gardens in Sturtevant.

Kilbourn Gardens

Those born before 1970 might remember the towering Kilbourn Gardens sign and huge martini glass that beckoned road-weary travelers to the Highway 20 exit off I-94. Its humble beginnings go back to 1925 when it was a roadside stand known as Beebe's Barbecue, owned by William "Beebe" Lencioni, a most colorful and trouble-prone character from Kenosha.

Lencioni was born in 1895. By his early twenties, he had already been apprehended numerous times for running moonshine, driving while intoxicated, speeding, and carrying a concealed weapon—sometimes all at once. He was once accused of mashing after he drunkenly harassed a young lady from his car as she walked down the street. The punishment was usually a hefty fine, or the charges were later dropped; he never did any jail time.

Somehow, amid all that turmoil, he managed to open his namesake eatery, which was later renamed Kilbourn Gardens, after the lane that wound past the front door. Trouble continued to plague Lencioni; he and another man were badly burned when a propane gas tank they were changing exploded. The blast blew out the side of a small building next to Kilbourn Gardens. The injured pair managed to put out the fire with a garden hose just as the fire department arrived. Soon after, slot machines were discovered at his roadhouse, and Lencioni was brought up on state charges. In 1931, he was arrested yet again after federal agents found beer and whiskey being sold.

"BEEBE" SAYS HE DIDN'T OGLE LADY

She Says He Told Her to go to—, After She Refused to Ride.

BUT HE CLAIMS ALIBI

OLD SPONGE SQUAD GET MOON AT TWO RESORTS

LENCIONI SAYS HE HAD "REAL STUFF"

Won't Plead Guilty to Having Moonshine — Case of Mashing Against Him Dismissed — Driving While Intoxicated Case Continued.

Two headlines from 1922

Aerial image of
Kilbourn Gardens,
1964 COURTESY OF
VINTAGEAERIAL.COM

Habitually tempted by the easy money to be made selling illegal liquor, Lencioni was arrested on a prohibition law charge one more time before he died in a car crash in Morocco, Indiana, in January 1935. Lencioni's wife Marie, who survived the accident, took over the operation of Kilbourn Gardens. A year later, she was fined for having slot machines again. By 1943, she had remarried and decided to sell Kilbourn Gardens to John Shemkus, who had been the manager and head chef at the Kilbourn Country Club for eight years. Barely seven months into Shemkus's tenure, Kilbourn Gardens was raided; this time, five slot machines were confiscated. In February 1945, the Milwaukee Office of Price Administration (OPA) suspended Shemkus for the duration of the war for dealing in rationed meats on the black market. An OPA commissioner ruled that the suspension be eased on all commodities except beef after Shemkus repaid 16,365 ration points.

A much more serious disaster struck in May of 1947 when an explosion blew apart the roadhouse and completely leveled the building. Ten people were hurt in the blast, including John, his wife Clara, a waitress, and several patrons. The damage was estimated at $60,000. The cause was thought to be a butane tank that was struck by lightning during a powerful thunderstorm. Kilbourn Gardens was rebuilt as a modern supper club and reopened for New Year's Eve that year. However, just nine months later, another explosion occurred in a stone block structure behind the main building.

THE OPA DURING WORLD WAR II

To help support the American effort in World War II, President Franklin Delano Roosevelt created the Office of Price Administration in April of 1941. The purpose of the OPA was to control prices and prevent profiteering and

hoarding. Rationing was implemented for commodities like tires, gasoline, oil, and automobiles, as well as canned foods, meat, coffee, butter, and sugar. Households and restaurant owners were issued monthly ration books for these items, and a point system limited what they were able to purchase. In 1943, a homemaker wanting to pay for a twenty-ounce can of corn needed to use fourteen points, *plus* the cost of the item, since ration points were not actual money. Without the points, she wasn't able to buy the corn. Restaurants had similar limitations, although they received higher food allotments to allow for waste. Needless to say, many were dissatisfied with the regulations. In addition to limiting food and other necessary supplies, the ration books and procedures changed constantly, which was confusing for consumers. Restrictions led to a thriving black market where both private citizens and restaurant owners generally found what they needed—if they were able to pay the exorbitant prices. According to the US Department of Agriculture, 20 percent of all meat found its way into the black market during World War II.

Restaurant proprietors were additionally burdened with ceiling price limits of 8 percent over cost. As a result, menus were printed with a notification: "All prices are our ceiling prices or below. By OPA regulation, our ceilings are based on our highest prices from [seven-day period]. Our menus or price lists for that week are available for your inspection." Some menus also listed other conditions, such as: "No substitutions of rationed foods," "Rationed meats are not available at all times," and "Kindly ascertain from the waiter what can be had before ordering."

As people began dining out more because of war work or ration limits at home, restaurant owners often found that table items like ketchup bottles and sugar cubes disappeared in their customers' pockets. Furthermore, they faced sanctions from the OPA if they sold black market goods or set prices that exceeded the ceiling limits. In the summer of 1945, one supper club owner in Miami was hit with a $15,040 penalty (approximately $216,000 in 2020) when investigators found that he had sold bourbon and Scotch drinks at 8 percent over ceiling prices and other mixed drinks at 30 percent over the ceiling price.

While rationing ended in September of 1945, the OPA continued to oversee post-war price controls until it was disbanded in May of 1947.

This time it was caused by a gas leak accidentally ignited by a lit paper torch held by John Shemkus, who sustained severe burns on his face, hands, arms, and legs. After undergoing a number of skin grafting operations, he survived. This time, the Sturtevant community rallied to cover his medical bills with a fundraising drive led by the Sturtevant Athletic Club.

By 1949, the Shemkuses had brought in Roy and Selma Tischendorf as partners. Shortly afterward, a new kitchen was installed, and more space was added to the dining room. Unfortunately, just two years later, Roy Tischendorf died unexpectedly at age forty-seven. In July 1955, John Shemkus suffered a fatal heart attack at the club. He was sixty-five.

With the aid of Roy's son Roger, who had become the general manager, a $35,000 remodeling project was unveiled in March of 1964. It featured a new bar with a waterfall feature, new dining room fixtures and lighting, and an enhanced entrance to the building. It was the first major renovation since Kilbourn Gardens was rebuilt after the fire in 1947. The remodeling began a new chapter, as US 41 had been transformed into I-94. As more people traveled between Chicago and Milwaukee, as well as to their cabins and cottages in the Northwoods, there was an increase in traffic to the area. Kilbourn's fried chicken subsequently became a popular carryout item for road trips.

After Clara Shemkus retired in 1967, Roger and Selma offered live lobster dinners and Door County fish boils three nights a week. During Lent, they hosted the Kilbourn Klambake, which featured a seafood buffet with salads, relishes, oysters, shrimp, and *hors d'oeuvres*. All this was in addition to the regular menu of steaks, chops, fresh fish, and their famous cabbage salad. In the fall of 1973, another major renovation

MERRY CHRISTMAS   HAPPY NEW YEAR

SELMA *AND* ROY TISCHENDORF   CLARA *AND* JOHN SHEMKUS

Kilbourn Gardens' renovation illustration, 1973; Kilbourn postcard, circa late 1950s

enlarged the dining area by more than one hundred seats. A new, larger, circular bar area was installed, along with bigger restrooms, a new lobby, and a gift shop. The most noticeable addition was a sixty-foot-tall, illuminated sign and martini glass, which towered over the landscape. The grand reopening was held in April 1974.

However, the expansion came a little too late; by that time, fast food chains had already begun to move into the area. In addition, people's attitudes toward drinking had started to change as stricter drunk driving laws were enacted. Eventually, the Tischendorfs put Kilbourn Gardens up for sale. In early 1981, the IRS padlocked the property for liens over unpaid taxes for the previous two years.

In May of the same year, Mike Ress and his wife Anna, owners of the Colony Inn next door, as well as Colony East in Racine, purchased the property for more than $500,000. However, their ownership was troubled from the start; their liquor license was suspended for ten days in December over license and code violations. In May 1984, they were temporarily shut down by the health department over unsanitary conditions in the kitchen. Confusing name changes further damaged business, and by 1997, the property was scheduled for a sheriff's auction. The building was eventually demolished and replaced by a gas station in 2005.

Ray Bussler's

Ten miles north of Kilbourn Gardens, on the northeast corner of Highway 41 (27th Street) and Oakwood Road, was the White Manor Inn. It was originally established in the late 1800s as Yacky's Tavern, a wagon trail rest stop on what was then called Kilbourn Road. In 1946, Ray Albert Bussler, a former tackle for the Chicago Cardinals professional football team and a WWII naval officer, purchased the property and opened Ray Bussler's White Manor Inn. He eventually shortened the name to Ray Bussler's. It should be noted that Ray also owned two other properties along Highway 41—Longacres, which was south of Rawson Avenue on the east side of the street, and the 9 Mile Inn, which was near White Manor Inn. All three featured drinks, dining, dancing, and room for private parties and weddings.

The supper club soon became a popular stop for steaks and family-style meals. Bussler was known to be a bit of a perfectionist; he required waitresses to wear a pressed uniform, have clean nails, neatly brushed hair, and no runs in their nylons. Customers enjoyed the complimentary cheddar cheese spread, crackers, and breadsticks served at the large, curved bar, along with generously poured drinks. At the table, a lazy Susan with an assortment of vegetables preceded dinner, along with soup and salad.

In addition to menu choices of steak, seafood, and chops, all-you-can-eat family-style meals were served with a choice of meats and sides. For many customers, it felt like dining at home. After dinner, a complimentary tray of cordials (usually peppermint schnapps) was placed at the table, along with a fruit basket filled with apples, grapes, oranges, and tangerines, plus a bowl of butterscotch candies.

Unfortunately, in October of 1969, Ray died at the rather young age of fifty-four after suffering a heart attack on a trip to Granite City, Illinois. His wife Ann and his son Ray, Jr. continued to run the supper club; Ray, Jr. retired in 2005. It was posted for sale, but by then, the location and building were long past their prime; the former supper club was eventually demolished and remains a weed-covered lot across from St. John's Lutheran Church.

Ray Bussler's advertisement, 1962

CHUMP CHANGE

For those interested in glimpsing what Ray Bussler's looked like back in the day, watch the 2000 film *Chump Change*, written and directed by Steve Burrows; it was partially shot at the supper club. Burrows, a former resident of Greendale, stars in the Miramax movie along with Traci Lords, Tim Matheson, Fred Willard, and Jerry Stiller. "Ray Bussler's was the *only* supper club we ever went to. It was for very special occasions only—graduations, big birthdays," recalls Burrows. "It was such a unique, singular place that when I had the opportunity to make a film, I knew instantly I wanted to shoot there, as I had never seen a supper club like that in a movie. I remember taking my New York producer, Mary Anne Page, to dinner there to scout the location, and she instantly fell in love with everything about it—the look, the presentation of the food, the whole experience. That night we approached Ray, Jr. and locked in our first location for *Chump*. Bussler's set the bar for the rest of the locations in the film. We wanted to make sure every single location we used was of Wisconsin, and like no other place." Burrows also filmed the movie's winter scenes five miles north of Bussler's at the 41 Twin Drive-In before it, too, was demolished and replaced by the campus of Northwestern Mutual Insurance in 2004.

Steve Burrows
and Traci Lords
at Ray Bussler's
COURTESY OF
MIRAMAX AND
STEVE BURROWS

Rafters and DiMiceli's Rafters

OAK CREEK • 1960 TO 2010

Rafters was opened by Joseph Dimiceli and his son Frank in 1960. Located south of Rawson Avenue on 27th Street and several miles north of Ray Bussler's, the building was once a rather seedy motel. It was transformed by the Dimicelis into a cocktail lounge and restaurant, and the motel was made more family friendly. Joseph had been in the restaurant business since 1919 and had owned Dimiceli's Top of the Town restaurant on 22nd Street and West Wells Street for thirty years. Sadly, just three years after opening Rafters, he passed away at the age of sixty-nine. With his son Frank in charge, Rafters became a destination for top-flight steaks, which were broiled over a charcoal grill situated in the dining room. The menu offered classic supper club fare along with Italian pasta dishes as entrées or sides. Allegedly, Frank Sinatra was a good friend of the family and usually stopped by for dinner and a card game when he was in town.

In the 1970s, Frank DiMiceli (he spelled it with a capital M) was often the high bidder on the grand champion steer at the Wisconsin State Fair. In 1975, he paid $18,000 for it, then hosted a steak dinner with the beef at DiMiceli's Rafters as a benefit for the Special Olympics. The next year, he donated the prize steer to St. Mary's Hill Hospital to be used in fundraising drives for its child-adolescent treatment program.

After a fire in May of 1985 severely damaged the dining room and motel, DiMiceli considered closing, but he ultimately decided to rebuild because of the speculation that a new Brewers baseball stadium would be located on some of the available land nearby. Unfortunately for DiMiceli's Rafters, and the other hopeful businesses in the area, the new ballpark was instead built

Fire at DiMiceli's Rafters, 1985

next to the old County Stadium. During the renovation, DiMiceli purchased the Black Steer along with his colleagues Jerry Arenas and Tom Miller. The restaurant was located on the corner of Highway 100 and West Greenfield Avenue. DiMiceli later left the partnership, and Arenas and Miller renamed it Steak House 100. In 1987, DiMiceli's Charhouse opened in the former Layton Place Supper Club on 43rd Street and West Layton Avenue (now Los Mariachis Mexican Restaurant). It featured seafood and live music. Frank DiMiceli passed away in 1993 at the age of 74. The club continued to operate under family ownership until the spring of 2010 when a sign on the door announced a temporary closing due to "an emergency." It never reopened.

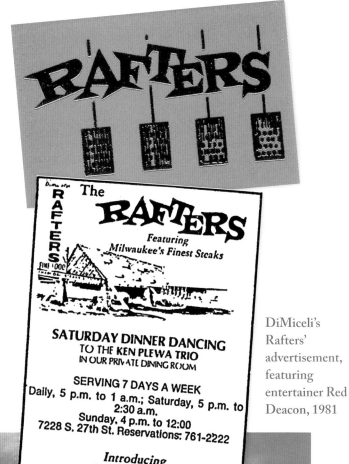

DiMiceli's Rafters' advertisement, featuring entertainer Red Deacon, 1981

Three Cellars Wine moved into the empty Rafters building after extensive remodeling in 2017 and doubled as a bar and retail store. It closed two years later.

Security National Bank, Sheboygan, Wis.

Chapter 11

THINGS WILL BE GREAT WHEN YOU'RE ... DOWNTOWN

Supper clubs in Wisconsin weren't limited to the rural roadhouses and Northwoods outposts. In urban areas, office buildings hosted some long-time favorites. The advantage for the clubs was that the buildings offered a built-in customer base that didn't have to worry about parking or weather. It also helped that office parties and meetings could be held in the club's banquet rooms and private dining rooms. In addition, maintenance of the building and surrounding grounds was taken care of, and in some cases, diners had a nice view of nature, sunsets, city-scapes, and lakefronts.

Juneau Hotel, Milwaukee, Wis.

Eugene's Sea Food
MILWAUKEE • 1924 TO 1974

Most people will remember Eugene's location inside the Travelers Building on the southeast corner of Wisconsin Avenue and Cass Street. What they may not realize is that it was a landmark destination for five decades and was originally located in the Hotel Juneau on the very same spot (more or less). Eugene's was just one block west of the Chicago and North Western Railway depot on Milwaukee's lakefront. Upon seeing the shimmering water of the lake and the giant neon lobster hovering over the hotel's entrance, new arrivals at the station might think they were in Maine instead of Milwaukee. And they weren't disappointed, as Eugene's dished up lobster twelve different ways: broiled, boiled, *à la* Newburg, Thermidor. Shrimp, oysters, clams, and crab were also available, along with whitefish, fresh lake trout, crayfish, fried chicken, and prime rib. Appetizers included Beluga caviar and shrimp *de Jonghe* (a Chicago recipe not usually seen on Milwaukee menus). A special late-night menu featured a hot brown sandwich (an open-faced turkey and bacon sandwich topped with creamy Mornay sauce, created at the Brown Hotel in Louisville, Kentucky), Welsh rarebit (a kind of melted cheese sandwich), omelets with crab or chicken livers, a Monte Cristo sandwich, cheese blintzes, and a Milwaukee favorite, steak tartare with onion, raw egg, and capers.

Above: Juneau Hotel and C&NW train station, 1915

Eugene's was the namesake of Eugene Trimberger, who was born in Sheboygan in 1883. At the age of twelve, he relocated to Milwaukee and began his restaurant career in the kitchen of the Milwaukee Club. It was an elite fraternity of local banking, commercial, and industrial circles, which included among its illustrious members some prominent family names, such as Layton, Plankinton, Allis, Uihlein, Bradley, Ilsley, Pfister, Wells, and Pabst. When he was fifteen, he volunteered to fight in the Spanish-American War and was taken prisoner. While this seems trivial and somewhat doubtful, it's worth mentioning only because the rallying cry of "Remember the Maine!" may have inspired his decision to open a lobster restaurant. As it was, upon his return home, he returned to his kitchen duties at the Milwaukee Club and, at age twenty-two, was promoted to manager. By 1924, he had purchased the Juneau Hotel (as it was called then) and opened Eugene's Sea Food in the space formerly occupied by the Juneau Buffet and Juneau Lunch coffee shop. (This part of the city was formerly Juneau Town, named for Solomon Juneau, the founder of Milwaukee.) Trimberger, ever loyal to his hometown, completely refurbished the hotel and restaurant with goods made by Sheboygan companies, including plumbing fixtures by Kohler. Despite being occupied with running the hotel and restaurant, he was somehow able to continue managing the Milwaukee Club. True-blue club members often made the short walk east to dine at Eugene's place, despite other nearby options.

Eugene's, 1959

In 1948, Trimberger retired due to his ailing health. He sold the hotel and restaurant to Maurice Berger. Trimberger passed away less than a year later. In 1954, disaster struck when a kitchen fire caused $80,000 in damages; the repairs forced Eugene's to close for more than a month. By 1962, head chef Morris "Mokie" Friedman became the third owner, but his tenure was interrupted when the Hotel Juneau was purchased, demolished, and replaced by a nine-story office building (now called Juneau Square North). It became the Milwaukee headquarters of Travelers Insurance; their trademark red umbrella sign replaced Eugene's giant neon lobster. During construction, Friedman spent two years as the Pfister Hotel's director of catering and brought with him his favorite recipes from Eugene's, which were featured in the Pfister's English Room.

When Eugene's reopened on the ground floor of the office building in 1966, Friedman retained ownership but hired Joel Reinstein to manage the restaurant. By this time, train travel had diminished, and the C&NW depot was scheduled to be demolished to make way for a proposed Lake Freeway. The final train rolled into the station in May 1966, and the depot was bulldozed two years later. However, the Lake Freeway was never built. Still, Eugene's remained a popular dining destination for several years. In 1971, construction began on the property across Cass Street at 777 East Wisconsin Avenue for what became the state's tallest building, the First Wisconsin Center (now the US Bank Center). Despite the construction traffic and road closures, Eugene's stayed open until 1974, when Friedman decided to close. In 1975, a high-end French café called Jean-Paul Restaurant Français opened for business, run by chef Jean-Paul Weber. However, since the 1990s, the space has been occupied by a private office.

Eugene's postcard, circa 1930s

Entrees

LOBSTER AND CRAB

WHOLE MAINE LOBSTER
Broiled or Boiled
BROILED MAINE LOBSTER,
Stuffed with Crabmeat or Shrimp Newburg

> Depending on size and current market. Please check with waitress.

Lobster Thermidor	4.00
Maine Lobster Thermidor	6.50
MAINE LOBSTER THERMIDOR AU GRATIN Service for Two	12.00
Lobster Maurice	5.75
Lobster a la Newburg	4.25
Maine Lobster a la Newburg	6.00
Lobster Tail, Broiled, Boiled or French Fried	5.00
ALASKAN KING CRAB LEGS, Broiled or Cold	4.50
Crabmeat Au Gratin	3.50
Deviled Crab	3.00
PACIFIC COAST CRAB, Broiled or Cold	4.00
Soft Shelled Crabs, Sautéed or French Fried	4.75
Lobster Petite	4.00
Cold Maryland Crabmeat Lumps, Drawn Butter	4.25
CRAB JEZEBEL	4.25

FROM LAKES, SEAS AND STREAMS

Abalone Steak Sauté fine herbes	4.50
COLORADO BROOK TROUT Broiled or Sautéed in Butter	4.25
EUGENE'S 7-SEAS SEA FOOD PLATTER, Shrimp, Scallops, Oyster, Frog Leg, Red Snapper, Deviled Crab and Lobster Tail	3.95
Filet of Lemon Sole	2.75
IMPORTED ENGLISH SOLE, Sauté Amondine	4.25
Finnan Haddie, Steamed or Delmonico	2.75
Baby Frog Legs, Sauté or French Fried	3.75
Jumbo Frog Legs, Sauté or French Fried	4.75
Butter Fried Lake Perch	2.50
Lake Superior Trout, Broiled	4.00
Oregon Halibut Steak	3.00
POMPANO EN PAPILLOTE	5.95
Broiled Florida Pompano	4.95
Red Snapper, Broiled or Boiled	4.25
Poached Snapper Antoinette	6.25
SNAPPER ALA LESTER	5.75
Turbot, Broiled or Sauté	4.50
Salmon Steak	3.00
Shad Roe and Bacon, Broiled or Sautéed	4.50
Smelts, French Fried or Sautéed	2.25
Swordfish Steak	3.00
Swordfish Steak Planked for Two	6.00
PLANKED STUFFED FLOUNDER VIEUX CARRE	4.95
Wall Eyed Pike, French Fried, Sautéed or Broiled	3.75
Lake Superior Whitefish, Broiled	4.00

SHRIMP OYSTERS SCALLOPS

Louisiana Shrimp Creole	3.00
French Fried Shrimp	2.85
Shrimps Sauté Meuniere or Provencale	3.50
Shrimp a la Newburg	3.50
Shrimp de Jonghe	3.50
Shrimp Curry with Rice	3.75
GIANT GUAYMAS SHRIMP, Sautéed or French Fried	3.50
Oysters, French Fried	2.50
Deep Sea Scallops, French Fried or Sautéed	2.75
Bay Scallops, Sautéed or French Fried	3.50
Broiled Shrimp, a la Jackson, Wild Rice	3.50
SHRIMP TEMPURA	3.00

STEAKS AND CHOPS

Roast Prime Ribs of Beef, Au Jus	4.75
Pullman Cut	6.50
Sirloin Strip Steak, N. Y. Cut	6.00
Eugene's Special Prime Filet Mignon	5.25
Ground Chopped Steak Deluxe, Onion and Mushroom Sauce	2.50
PLANKED GROUND SIRLOIN IMPERIAL	4.00
Double French Lamb Chops (2) with Mint Jelly	4.50
Pork Chops (2) with Apple Sauce	3.75
Wiener Schnitzel	3.00
Wiener Schnitzel a la Holstein	3.25
Tenderloin and Mushrooms en Brochette	2.75
Double Sirloin Strip, Planked — Service for Two	14.00
Beef Strogonoff	4.25
Braised or Creamed Sweetbreads with Mushrooms	3.00
Sweetbreads a la Mornay	3.50

POULTRY AND GAME

Milkfed Chicken, Broiled or Southern Fried	2.50
BONED WHOLE BABY CHICKEN, Wild Rice	4.25
BREAST OF CAPON, Princess Eugenié	5.00
Chicken a la King	3.50
Roast Long Island Duckling, Wild Rice Dressing	4.25
Chicken Livers en Brochette	2.50
Chicken Livers Sautéed, with Sherry Wine & Mushrooms	3.25
Roast Turkey and Wild Rice en Casserole	3.50
Braised Pheasant with Wild Rice	7.00
ROCK CORNISH GAME HEN, Wild Rice	5.50
Baked Squab, Wild Rice	5.75
Curried Chicken, Chutney	4.00

TOSSED SALAD, ROLLS, BUTTER AND FRENCH FRIED, BOILED OR MASHED POTATOES SERVED WITH ENTREES.

ASK WAITRESS FOR COMPLETE WINE LIST

Eugene's

Eugene's menu, circa late 1960s COURTESY OF MILWAUKEE COUNTY HISTORICAL SOCIETY

Benedict's Heidelberg Club, Sky Garden, Geno's Top of the First, City Streets

The tallest office building in Sheboygan is currently home to US Bank, but when it was built in 1922, it was the Security National Bank building. Originally established by James H. Mead in 1856 as The German Bank, it became the Security National in 1918. Architectural plans for the new building called for the top two floors to house a businessmen's club for the Sheboygan Association of Commerce. The sixth floor had a card room and billiard room along with offices. The seventh floor was known as the Roof Garden and contained a main dining hall and three smaller dining rooms, all with vaulted ceilings and terrazzo floors. Doors to the four rooms could be opened to create one large banquet hall seating more than 400 people. The north side of the building contained the kitchen, bake shop, pantry, refrigeration, dishwasher, storage, and waiters' locker room. The west and south side had a promenade extending around the full length of the building, providing views of the city and cooling breezes in the summer.

In December 1933, after the Association's ten-year lease expired, the seventh floor became Benedict's Heidelberg Club. Owner William B. Benedict was born in Switzerland and was once a chef for Emperor Franz Joseph of Austria. After serving as chef in the Café de Paris in Paris and the Ritz-Carlton in both London and New York City, he moved to Neenah in 1929. There he was the head chef at the North Shore Golf Club. The Heidelberg Club offered dining and dancing in rooms decorated in gold and red damask. The walls of the lobby had eight oil paintings depicting German scenes, including the Heidelberg court and Heidelberg castle. A new bar was built on the east end of the dining room, and a draped orchestra stage with subdued lighting was installed. Cocktail hour was daily from 4:00 p.m. to 6:00 p.m., and cocktails were twenty-five cents. The menu featured southern fried chicken, Maine lobsters, and "Blue Ribbon" steaks.

Benedict retired in 1945 after selling the club to Rudolph Wegner of Sheboygan. Four years later, Wegner sold the club to Robert Powers, who renamed it the Powers Club Heidelberg Restaurant. It featured the relatively new Muzak (which was later

Opposite:
Sky Garden
interior, circa
1950s

BENEDICT'S HEIDELBERG CLUB, SHEBOYGAN, WISCONSIN

Benedict's Heidelberg Club, the show-place of the northwest, is a truly beautiful rendezvous for the citizens and tourists of Sheboygan. The beauty of atmosphere and the grandeur of setting is matched only by the delicious food and drink as served by the Heidelberg competent staff.

scorned as "elevator music") piped into the dining rooms. Powers eventually moved on, and in November 1952, Carl and Otto Horner took over as new owners of what they called the Sky Garden. The brothers were born in Leipzig, Germany, and worked in several European restaurants before they arrived in Milwaukee in 1925. Prior to the Sky Garden, Carl was executive chef at the Plankington House, and Otto was the auxiliary chef at the University Club in Milwaukee. Extensive renovations were done on the Sky Garden, including new honey-blond woodwork, a warm color scheme on the walls, new draperies and linens, leafy green plants, and an updated, streamlined bar. Carl bought out Otto's interest in the club in the late 1950s, and by the end of 1963, he decided to retire at the age of seventy-one.

After three months of negotiations, Gene A. Korman, formerly of Hoffman's at Riverdale, purchased the Sky Garden and reopened the restaurant in January 1964 as Geno's Gracious Sky Club. It offered live music and dancing, and a Sunday brunch and smorgasbord were later added to the regular menu. In the spring of 1967, the bank was renamed Security First National, and the building, along with Geno's, underwent substantial remodeling. The exterior of the building was covered in Spandrelite, a contemporary, black curtain wall façade. The seventh floor was gutted and rebuilt, including the installation of all-new equipment and furnishings. During the construction, Korman held a contest to rename the club, and Geno's Penthouse opened to great fanfare in June of 1967. Within a month, the name mysteriously changed to Geno's Top of the First. Even so, it remained a popular nightspot in Sheboygan through 1984, when it became City Streets restaurant. Sometime after City Streets closed in 1990, the seventh floor was turned into offices, ending a seventy-year run of good food with a great view.

Eve's Supper Club

t first glance, the office building along the river in Allouez seems to be a very unlikely place for a supper club. The Brutalist design is cold and unwelcoming and reinforced by narrow, black-tinted windows; the effect suggests a secret government bunker or laboratory, and yet for forty years, it was the home to one of Green Bay's most beloved places to dine out.

The first location for Eve's Supper Club was at 1928 Riverside Drive, in a small building that was formerly home to the Shrimp Shack, Paddy's Pig, and the Shore-Lite Supper Club. It was opened by Eve and Randy Haltaufderheid in 1967. Eve was a waitress at the Golden Inn just down the street, and Randy was a highway engineer. They decided to take a chance and open their own restaurant. At the start, the restaurant had just twelve tables and ten employees, but the gamble paid off because within five years, they were ready for a larger space, which just happened to be next door. When the Haltaufderheids opened for business at 2020 Riverside Drive on Friday, October 13, 1972, they had three times more room and views of the tree-lined Fox River. The third-floor supper club featured the Hearthside Room, with a black-mirrored fireplace and room for a hundred people, and the Treetop room, which seated fifty people and was decorated in olive and brown. Eve and Randy's sons both worked at the club; Jerry was the head bartender, and Rick was the head chef. The staff wore clean, neatly pressed uniforms. The supper club served favorites such as prime rib and Grandma Anna Haltaufderheid's chicken soup. Packer specials were served during football season, and Eve's even provided bus service to and from home games at Lambeau Field. In the 1980s, on their busiest nights, Eve's served around 350 dinners. Among the most popular dishes were crab legs, stuffed flounder, and baked scallops. Randy died in 1997, and Eve followed in 2002. Rick and Jerry carried on operations until the club closed abruptly on July 1, 2013. It was a surprise to staff and customers, as there had been no prior warning. The contents of Eve's were sold at auction a couple of months later, putting to rest any speculation that the club would reopen.

Football Special - Serving Before & After Game
BUS SERVICE TO AND FROM THE GAME — Open 11 A.M. Daily Serving 5 to 10:30 P.M.

Cover
CHARGE
$1.50
PER PERSON

BILTM◌
One of Americ◌

Cover
CHARGE
$1.00
PER PERSON

BILTMORE *Bowl*
One of America's Truly Fine Supper Clubs

Chapter 12
IT'S SHOW TIME!

Supper club entertainment was an essential part of a night out, whether it was dancing to a live orchestra or jazz band or a kind of variety show with singing, dancing, and comedy. As theaters transitioned from offering vaudeville shows to movies in the 1930s, performers turned to the supper club circuit for work. Radio, and later television, became new outlets for exposure, which led to more gigs and better paydays. Even the small regional acts found plenty of steady work. It was the golden age of live entertainment in clubs.

Below is an introduction to four Wisconsin-born supper club entertainers who worked during the second half of the twentieth century. All four were uniquely gifted individuals who enjoyed varying levels of fame and fortune. Two were known for their fashionable elegance (even if it was a bit over the top), yet they each dealt with their star status differently. The other two found fame on a smaller scale by using their creative skills to entertain and earn a good living.

Hildegarde

Hildegarde Loretta Sell, known professionally as Hildegarde, was born in 1906 in the tiny village of Adell in Sheboygan County. When she was six months old, her parents, Charles and Ida, moved north to New Holstein, where they ran a grocery store. In 1918, the Sell family moved to the Washington Park neighborhood of Milwaukee, where she sang in the school choir and studied piano at the School of Music at Marquette University. As a teenager, she attended St. John's Cathedral High School and had a part-time job at Gimbels department store, which was located downtown. Her mother helped her find a job at the Lyric Theater on 38th Street and Vliet Street, where she played the piano accompaniment to silent movies. Between films, she sat cross-legged in the lobby, dressed up in beads and veils to promote The Sheik, starring Rudolph Valentino. Hildegarde later claimed her experience at the Lyric Theater gave her the confidence to overcome her acute shyness in front of people. The five dollars she earned per week went toward tuition and books.

With a newfound ambition to entertain (and contribute to the family's finances), she went to see a vaudeville act called *Jerry and Her Baby Grands* at the Palace Theater on 6th Street and Wisconsin Avenue. Onstage, four girls dressed in white and wearing white wigs played "Stars and Stripes Forever" on white, baby grand pianos with illuminated keyboards. She was thrilled with the show, and when it was over, she went backstage to ask Jerry for a job playing piano. After auditioning with "Twelfth Street Rag," she was hired to tour the country in a junior version of the act for seventy-five dollars a week, half of which she sent back home to her parents.

Hildegarde eventually landed in New York City's vaudeville scene and was hired by impresario Gus Edwards. Years later, she appeared in one of his revues at the Riverside Theater in Milwaukee. He was the first to determine she should be known only by her first name; however, it was Anna Sosenko who ignited Hildegarde's career. The two became friends when Hildegarde stayed at a theatrical boarding house in Camden, New Jersey, run by Sosenko's mother. Sosenko, who was three years younger, was at one time a reporter for the *Philadelphia Inquirer* and wanted to become a songwriter. She was described by the *Brooklyn Gazette* as a "short, stocky, aggressive-looking brunette." Sosenko created, packaged, promoted, and managed Hildegarde's career. She also wrote the music and lyrics for more than fifteen songs, including "Darling, *Je Vous Aime Beaucoup*," Hildegarde's signature tune.

The pair eventually moved to London, then Paris. All the while, they worked to refine Hildegarde's energetic and glamorous performances in nightclubs across Europe. Upon their return to the United States in 1936, Hildegarde was a star; she appeared on several top-ten radio shows produced by Sosenko, including *99 Men and a Girl*, *Beat the Band*, and *Supper Club of the Air: The Raleigh Room*. In April 1939, her portrait graced the cover of *Life* magazine.

She was one of the highest-paid entertainers in the 1940s; reportedly, she earned $150,000 in a single year (in 1948, she earned $7,500 per week at the Cocoanut Grove in Los Angeles). Journalist Walter Winchell dubbed her "The Incomparable Hildegarde," which became her trademark; he also said she was "the dear that made Milwaukee famous." (In addition, George and Ira Gershwin's song, "My Cousin in Milwaukee," was said to be inspired by her.) Hildegarde's ambitious touring schedule kept her on the road at least forty-five weeks each year. She traveled with her own orchestra and several dozen pieces of luggage, including 200 pairs of the full-length gloves that she wore while on stage.

In 1947, she made a triumphant return to her birthplace for a performance and later began her tours in the Badger State. When asked by *Brooklyn Daily Eagle* reporter Margaret Mara about her Parisian-Midwestern accent, she replied, "I always talked like this! My whole family in Milwaukee talks like this!"

When she wasn't touring, she lived with Anna Sosenko in a ten-room apartment in the Plaza Hotel in Manhattan. While they were equal partners in business, it is unknown whether that partnership was also romantic. It is possible that the relationship remained platonic, given Hildegarde's deeply religious convictions. When asked about why she remained single, Hildegarde said she "met a lot of men and had a lot of romances, but it never worked out. It was always 'Hello and goodbye.'" Onstage she was a noted flirt and passed out long-stemmed roses to the men in the audience. She once bristled at a comment that Sosenko was her Svengali: "What Anna did—and it was great—was help me bring out my latent qualities. With no written agreement, we shared my earnings equally. Always—this was our plot—she was the business half of our firm. She dickered with the supper clubs, kept the books, decided where I would appear and where I would not appear. I was the artiste! Oh! My!" When she and Sosenko parted ways in 1955, Hildegarde later said, "My biggest gamble came, actually, when I was at the height of my success. With increasing money and prestige, Anna Sosenko had become bossier. And I had become resentful and rebellious. Our quarrels finally destroyed our relationship. And had we continued, I believe they would have destroyed us, too. Nevertheless, when we parted, as we had to, I was frightened. How

The curvy letter E at the end of Hildegarde's name signified a waving handkerchief.

Hildegarde's 7-inch EP, 1952;
Over 50…So What!, 1963

well would I do without Anna, so long my guide and mentor, I did not know." They were both very successful even after they parted ways; the two were briefly reunited before Sosenko's death in 2000.

Hildegarde continued to tour the lucrative supper club circuit for many years. She performed for four US presidents (Truman, Eisenhower, Kennedy, and Johnson) and made numerous television appearances. She released an autobiography, published by Doubleday, in 1963, called *Over 50 . . . So What!* In 1969, she paid a special tribute to her home state on *Hildegarde's Souvenir Record Album*, which featured the songs "My Milwaukee" and "Wisconsinland." The release was premiered during her concert in a high school auditorium in New Holstein that year. In 1992, when she was eighty-six, she appeared at the Performing Arts Center in Milwaukee. As a lifelong, devout Catholic, she passed away as a Third Order Carmelite nun in her New York home in 2005, at the age of ninety-nine. In the 1960s, Eleanor Roosevelt called her the "First Lady of Supper Clubs," a fitting tribute to her career. CD compilations of her songs and YouTube videos of her performances display the charismatic personality and glamorous stage show that was a major inspiration to another supper club entertainer from Wisconsin, Liberace.

Liberace

Indeed, the flamboyant showman incorporated some of Hildegarde's pizzazz into his own act, as he often opened for her in the early days of his career. Wladziu Valentino Liberace was born in 1919 in West Allis. When he was ten, his family moved to West Milwaukee, just south of National Avenue. His father, Salvatore "Sam" Liberace, was a musician and played French horn in the Milwaukee Symphony Orchestra. He also was a member of the orchestra that played at the Alhambra Theatre downtown, at 4th Street and Wisconsin Avenue, that featured vaudeville and silent movies. His mother, Frances, worked at the Johnston Cookie Company during the early 1930s. According to Liberace, she sometimes brought home a ten-pound sack of broken cookies from the factory. He and his sister Angie decorated them at Christmas—and ate plenty in the process. Sam encouraged his children to pursue musical education; by age four, Wladziu was a piano prodigy. Called "Walter" by his family and "Lee" by his friends, he began his musical education at the Wisconsin Conservatory of Music under the direction of Florence Bettray-Kelly. When he wasn't at the Conservatory, he often played piano for dance school classes and fashion shows. He also played for the soldiers at the National Veterans' Administration on National Avenue (now the Clement J. Zablocki Veterans Affairs Medical Center), which was located across the street from his home. As a teenager, he often snuck out of the house to play at Polish weddings and stag parties. He was once arrested, along with the other men at a stag party that featured nude dancers and pornographic movies. (He claims he lost his virginity to a prostitute at one of these parties.) When he and his band, The Mixers, were hired to play a silver wedding anniversary party at Sam Pick's Club Madrid, a bottle of gin was passed around. After taking several healthy swigs, Liberace passed out while playing "The Carioca."

When he was sixteen, he made his debut as a solo artist before the Society of Musical Arts in Chicago. (He later became a soloist with the Chicago Symphony Orchestra.) He was also hired to play piano on WTMJ Radio in Milwaukee. However, he was fired after he attempted to play a tune a little beyond his talent. Bettray-Kelly eventually talked the producers into hiring him back. With her help, he landed representation at a Chicago talent agency in 1938 and was sent on a tour of supper clubs around the Midwest. His agent came up with the stage name Walter Buster Keys on the theory that Walter Valentino Liberace sounded too high class. While

Liberace in concert, 1979

Liberace performing at the Manor Supper Club, North Wildwood, New Jersey, 1955

he performed under that name for less than a year, he was associated with it for the rest of his life.

In the 1940s, he began to tour with his older brother George, who accompanied him on violin and acted as the bandleader. Playing a unique mix of classical and pop music, their shows on the supper club circuit were well-attended. Liberace played a custom-made grand piano topped with his signature candelabra. The brothers' travels eventually took them to Hollywood, where Liberace appeared in his first film, *South Sea Sinner*, released in 1950 by Universal Studios. In the film, he played a Chopin tune on the piano to a rowdy crowd of sailors in a sleazy honky-tonk.

His next stop was television; he hosted *The Liberace Show*, a syndicated version of his supper club act. It became a big hit; it attracted 35 million viewers on average and aired from 1952 to 1959. While Liberace's flamboyant manner appealed to his predominantly female following, most were unaware or possibly didn't care that he was gay. When the *Daily Mirror*, a British tabloid, implied in a 1956 article that he was a homosexual, he sued the paper for libel. "[The article] has caused untold agonies and embarrassment and has made me the subject of ridicule," he said at the time. In June of 1959, a London jury of ten men and two women awarded Liberace damages of £8,000, or $22,400 (nearly $200,000 in 2020).

Possibly because of the publicity from the lawsuit, Liberace's career suffered a slump. He returned to the supper club circuit and made several television appearances, which helped turn things around. However, during an appearance in Pittsburgh in November of 1963, he suffered kidney failure from accidentally inhaling fumes from his just-dry-cleaned costumes. He survived. His next move proved to be one of his best.

Las Vegas was a still-sleepy desert town when Liberace first played there in 1944, but when he returned in the 1960s, it had transformed into a bustling city as glitzy and dazzling as his persona. His shows became more extravagant and his costumes more elaborate; he wore mink capes, large, jewel-encrusted rings, and flashy suits. He owned a lavish mansion and opened a supper club of his own, the Tivoli Gardens. In 1970, he released a cookbook, *Liberace Cooks! Recipes From His Seven Dining Rooms*. It featured "Liberace Lasagna," sticky buns, pierogi, sukiyaki, pasta sauces, and cookies. In his self-titled autobiography, published by Putnam in 1973, he addressed his status as a confirmed bachelor: "Should the right woman come along, one who clearly loves me enough to take a chance on me and I feel that deeply for her, I'm sure we'll both know that 'this is it.'"

He established the Liberace Foundation for the Performing and Creative Arts in 1976, which provided music scholarships for young artists at colleges across the United States. The non-profit is still in operation today, supported by the licensing income of the Liberace brand.

In the late 1970s, he continued to be a major box office draw in Vegas and Lake Tahoe and reportedly earned as much as $300,000 per week. He guest-starred on television's *The Muppet Show* and *Kojak*, and in 1985, made a cameo appearance in an episode of *Saturday Night Live*. During his travels, he returned to Milwaukee many times to play at the Performing Arts Center and Summerfest; he played his final series of shows at the Riverside Theatre in April of 1986. Throughout the 1980s, he suffered from heart disease and emphysema but eventually died of AIDS-related pneumonia on February 4, 1987, at sixty-seven. On the one-hundredth anniversary of his birth, the City of West Allis declared May 16, 2019 Liberace Appreciation Day. His high school alma mater, the West Milwaukee Intermediate School, renamed its main performance space the Liberace Auditorium.

Liberace FEATURED ON COLUMBIA RECORDS

PERSONAL MANAGEMENT
GABBE-LUTZ and HELLER
NEW YORK   HOLLYWOO

Liberace press photo, circa 1950s

Norbie Baker

At South 98th Street and West Dakota Street in West Allis, in the remnants of what was once Pleasant Valley Park, there was a supper club called Norbie Baker's Publick House. Owned by Norbie and Angie Baker, the Publick House was open Thursday through Sunday and was known for its prime rib served with *au jus* and whipped cream horseradish sauce.

The owner, Norbert Piekarski, was a Milwaukee polka legend from the 1950s. Piekarski was born in Milwaukee and began to play the accordion at the age of seven. After he graduated from Riverside High School, he anglicized his name to Baker and formed a polka band that toured the Midwest. In 1947, he teamed up with fellow Milwaukeean and banjo player Ralph "Gillie" Baddinger and recorded "Tinker Polka" and "La-La Waltz" as Norbie and Gillie, The Original Polka Boys, for Columbia Records. In 1953, now going by Norbie Baker and His Polka Boys, they released "Million Dollar Polka" and "Nightingale Waltz." Known as "Milwaukee's Frankie Yankovic," Baker continued to play dance halls, taverns, and church festivals.

Due to Rain Last Sunday

NORBIE BAKER
And His Columbia Recording Orchestra

re-scheduled to appear

**SUNDAY,
August 19**

1:00 to 5:00 p.m.

Sacred Heart Parish Grounds

End of State Street—Highway 38, Racine, Wis.

Saturday, August 18

*Barbecued Italian Sausage
Refreshments*

He also operated a tavern called the New Note at 2757 North 3rd Street. In 1950, he married Angie Osterman, and five years later, the couple opened Norbie Baker's Lounge at 4815 North Hopkins Street. The lounge featured a bar and dining room with a hall for dancing and private parties. When the building was sold in 1967, he and Angie launched the Publick House in a former tavern that was surrounded by suburban homes. The food was classic supper club fare, and the decor, designed by Angie, was Early American, with Delft plates along the walls and a large stone fireplace. The Publick House was able to seat eighty people, and as it became more popular, up to 300 dinners were served each night.

One of the regulars at Norbie Baker's was a fellow accordion player and polka bandleader, Jeff Winard. Winard toured with "America's Polka King" Frankie Yankovic from 1970 to 1997 and later continued to perform Yankovic's music with his own band. "I had known of Norbie and his music and Columbia Recordings," recalled Winard. "I did get to know him better when I had my bar (Winard's Adler Inn, on 71st and Adler). Norbie always loved the Slovenian/Yankovic music. He would come to my bar when I had bands on Sundays, and when I had Yankovic playing there. He asked me to stock Heineken beer! He liked the finer things. As far as a restauranteur, he wanted everything top notch: the best meats, liquor, ambiance, etc. The restaurant on Dakota had a very charming feel. He did much of the cooking, meat cutting, and other preparation duties."

As a touring musician himself, Winard often talked with Baker about those days on the road. "As with bands that were on national labels, the record companies wanted them to tour. As he got into the bar business, it was better to be 'home,' and he could play there as he had a good following. Of course, as with many others, family also kept musicians close to home. He did tell me he was not a fan of the traveling."

In 1988, Norbie and Angie decided to retire and closed the Publick House. They arranged for one last party to celebrate Norbie's forty-year career in music, entertainment, and dining. Baker asked Winard to lead the polka band that performed that night. "That final night was one of those times when you say, 'Why is this place closing?'" Winard recalled. "It was packed with many of his regulars and old friends, and many that knew him from his band days and early bars. He wanted to give his loyal customers something special. He was really a charming man." Norbie Baker passed away seven years later at the age of sixty-seven.

The site of Norbie Baker's Publick House in 2020. An empty lot with remnants of the sign.

(Clockwise from top) Norbie Baker matchbook, 1950; advertisement for polka show at Rustic Resort, 1955; Publick House advertisement, 1975

NORBIE BAKER'S
LOUNGE
DINING ROOM
AND HALL
4815 N. Hopkins St.
At Hampton

CLOSE COVER BEFORE STRIKING

"We're proud of the company we keep."

Dining and Cocktails

IT'S A FEW PLEASANT MILES TO DRIVE — BUT WELL WORTH THE TRIP

Your Hosts:
Angie and
Norbie Baker

Serving Thurs.-Sat.
5 to 10 P.M.
Sunday to 9 P.M.

ALL MAJOR CREDIT
CARDS ACCEPTED
Reservations 1-321-4321

Norbie Baker's
P U B L I C K   H O U S E

9801 W. DAKOTA ST. ● WEST ALLIS
Take I-94, then I-894. Exit at National Ave., go east one block
to 99th St., turn right (south) 5 blocks to Dakota St.

2 BANDS
For Your Dancing
Pleasure!
THURSDAY
JANUARY 13th
RUSTIC
● RESORT ●
CLINTONVILLE
(Between Clintonville
& Shawano on Hi Way 22)

IN PERSON
NORBIE BAKER
& His Orchestra
Columbia Recording Stars

In Person!
'America's Polka King'
FRANK
YANKOVIC
And His
Orchestra

Archie Ulm

"From Milwaukee, the 'Beer Capital,' to Colorado, the 'Ski Capital,' by way of the finest night spots the Midwest has to offer, Archie Ulm has devastated the traditional concept of organ playing by inciting his supper club audiences to stunning heights of musical awareness."

So goes the opening liner notes to *At the Yamaha EX-42*, an LP recorded by Milwaukee musician Archie Ulm in 1976. The album contains ten instrumental

tracks, including "The Hustle," "The Rockford Files Theme," "Harlem Nocturne," "Pink Panther," "Popcorn," and "The NBC Mystery Movie Theme." It was a popular souvenir for customers at the Steak Knife's two locations—at 117th and Bluemound Road and 13th Street and West College Avenue—during the 1970s and 1980s. Ulm's solo performances on his legendary Yamaha EX-42 organ kept the crowd entertained with classical music, big band, and rock and roll.

Ulm began taking accordion and organ lessons at the age of five. At sixteen, he joined his first rock band, The Traditions, a group with a regular gig at the Italian Village supper club on Jackson Street in the Third Ward. With the consent of his parents and a special permit from the city, he played the organ with the popular quintet five nights a week and attended school during the day. It was his first taste of fame. People lined up to get into the Italian Village's I.V. A-Go-Go Night to dance and see the band.

"It was scary sometimes because when you're sixteen and you got these guys in their late teens and early twenties and they get a little drunk—I didn't want to get my ass kicked," recalls Ulm. "Everyone kinda liked me because I was doing a

SIDE ONE		SIDE TWO	
THE HUSTLE	4:27	PINK PANTHER	4:23
IF	2:54	HOMECOMING	3:25
ROCKFORD FILES	2:55	POPCORN	3:55
HARLEM NOCTURNE	5:17	UNCHAINED MELODY	5:51
THE CAT	6:23	NBC MYSTERY MOVIE THEME	3:06

Cover photo by Dennis Sherfy

Ulm's self-released *At the Yamaha EX-42* LP, 1976

real good job. I was playing a portable organ, and at some point, I brought a Hammond B3 into the club—think of the Young Rascals song 'Good Loving'—and when the guys saw how well I could do the bass pedals, they fired the bass player. The group went from five guys to four guys, but I never got more money for it. [Laughs.] I'd be playing these simple little chords, but some of the bass parts were kinda intricate; I think that's what made me get really good at the bass pedal."

After missing too many school days because of the late-night shows, he accepted an offer to play the organ at Ruffini's restaurant in Brookfield. It was the beginning of his solo career. He later got a better offer to play at Alioto's on Alioto's on North Mayfair Road and West Burleigh Street. "I was a little bothered by some of the patrons there that got a little drunk," he says. He was then hired by George Krantz, the owner of the Steak Knife on Bluemound Road. Ulm remembers, "It was a dream come true for me. I would sign two-year contracts with Krantz for $600 per week. When I quit, I was making $800 a week, plus tips and record sales, which added another $200 a week. Sometimes customers would tip twenty bucks for me to play a song—that was a lot of money back then. I had enough money to go out to Colorado and camp out with my girlfriend. Having spent five to six nights a week in the clubs with a lot of people around me, it was nice to have some peace and quiet and nature.

"When I first started playing at the Steak Knife, they had an upstairs lounge, and I played in the main lounge downstairs. Paul Patterson played upstairs; he had more space for dancing. I was depressed when I started because more people would be upstairs. Then I was at Netzow's (a local music store), and they had the Yamaha EX-42; it was $17,000. I bought it and got proficient, and within a matter of weeks, the upstairs lounge at the Steak Knife was empty! [Laughs.] I can remember Paul on a break looking down at all the people by me and being upset that they weren't upstairs. [Laughs.]"

Besides Paul Patterson, Ulm remembers other supper club entertainers who were popular at the time. "Sonny's El Dorado—when I first started, there was a guy there named Tiny Maynard. Before Yamaha came out with these super modern instruments, the most modern one you could have was a Hammond X66, and Maynard had one. His wife Jessie would sing with him; they were a big attraction in the 1960s. She would also come to the Steak Knife and sing 'Hello Dolly' with me. Don LaRusso was a British guy, he played Alioto's organ bar. He was the first guy to use an automatic rhythm player. It was a big contraption, and the musician's union would picket Alioto's because this contraption was putting musicians out of work. [Laughs.] On the East Side, the jazz musicians don't like people who can read music, and vice versa. There was this guy, his name was Sig Millonzi, at that time he was in his fifties (Millonzi died at fifty-two). I went to hear him one time, and he played some jazz thing. He had a bass player and drummer with him, and when he announced the song, I didn't recognize it. It was 'Misty' (by Erroll Garner)."

Ulm began performing part-time in Fort Collins, Colorado, in 1973, after a patron got him a gig at the Ramada Inn. In the 1980s, he went into business at the Racine location of Billings Pianos and Organs but eventually moved permanently to Fort Collins, where he purchased thirty-six acres near the Roosevelt National Forest. He built a house on the property in 2000 and continues to record and play an occasional live show with his Yamaha ELX-1.

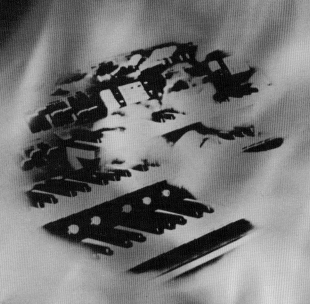

ARCHIE ULM EXPERIENCE!

album,
1, a
In-
ording
ters;
ond
the
Ulm,
on
ang-
lub
fter
re-

and complex for one man, Archie has recorded his second album, again displaying his extreme versatility by going from disco to country, to contemporary rock on one disc. Because Archie loves thrilling audiences of all ages, side 1 features him, backed by percussionist Paul Hergert, and steel guitarist Larry Carrico, while side 2 presents him as a soloist. Listen, and enjoy the experience.

	SIDE 2
* Time Is Tight	Clair De Lune
*After The Lovin'	MacArthur Park
* Caravan	Almost Like A
Help Me Make It Thru	Song
* the Night **	Bye-Bye Blues

Produced by: Joe Bastian + Archie Ulm
Engineered by: Ken Smith
Mixing: Ken Smith + Archie Ulm
Photography: Dennis Sherfy, Steve Evans
Percussion: Paul Hergert *
Steel Guitar: Larry Carrico **
Special Thanks To: Ronn Chow, John Clement, Mark Philipp, & Jim Ulm

Ulm's *Experience!* LP, 1979

Burger Chef's new Rancher Dinner.
For the man who's got a hunger for the taste of sirloin.

All the cool green salad you can eat.

Hearty ⅓ lb. of chopped beefsteak that's three-quarters sirloin— flame-broiled 'n pure delicious.

Crispy golden fries.

Hot Texas toast.

Only at Burger Chef.

Man, next time you get them down-home, tummy-growling hungries, get on over to Burger Chef and try our new Rancher Dinner. It's powerful big. And that sizzling sirloin taste—there ain't nothin like it. Nowhere!

The new Rancher Dinner. Only at Burger Chef.

Say, why not mosey in with the family and try it tonight?

There's <u>more</u> to like at Burger Chef.

OPEN 10:30 A.M.-11 P.M.   FRI.-SAT. 10:30 A.M.-1 A.M.

So don't settle for less.

S. 8th & Ind. Ave.

Chapter 13
STIFF COMPETITION

n the 1970s and '80s, supper clubs faced increased challenges from restaurant chains that imitated the supper club experience with a similar menu of steaks, seafood, cocktails, and in some cases, live entertainment and dancing. It may not have been a serious threat at first, but as the suburbs expanded and corporate eateries began popping up closer to the new subdivisions, it affected supper club business. Wisconsin chains included Nino's Steak Round-Up and Captain's Steak Joynt, and national chains included Mr. Steak, Ponderosa, Rustler, Sizzler, and Red Lobster, where high-end seafood dining was advertised as an "informal family-priced" dinner.

Fast food chains also offered cheaper versions of food found at the supper clubs, such as fish fry from Arthur Treacher's and fried chicken from the Kentucky Colonel. Even Shakey's Pizza Parlors had live entertainment, silent movies, and beer. A night out with the family cost less and was almost as much fun as a supper club, with absolutely no atmosphere. In addition, the corporate chains had huge advertising budgets and lower food costs from bulk purchasing.

These cookie-cutter concepts also meant that the same food could be found all over the country—a Big Mac in Milwaukee tasted the same as a Big Mac in Miami. This idea fit neatly into the era of space travel, fast cars, superhighways, instant breakfast, and microwave dinners. A second round of chains brought on even more competition from fast-casual places like Bennigan's, T.G.I. Friday's, Chili's, Applebee's, and the Ground Round, where the big thrill was throwing peanut shells on the floor. These faux supper clubs offered brand-new buildings, lively music, more affordable food, and, most importantly, well-stocked bars. However, with the increasingly strict drunk driving laws, customers at both supper clubs and chain restaurants cut back on their drinking and returned home earlier in the evening. In 1949, Wisconsin's standard for drunk driving was a blood alcohol concentration of .15 percent. In 1973, it was lowered to .1 percent, and in 1991, the legal limit became .08 percent. Supper clubs that used to be open until 1:00 or 2:00 a.m., or even later, began to close their kitchens at 9:00 p.m.

As the dawn of the internet presented new ways to promote businesses, supper club owners were slow to join in. As a result, they had little to no internet presence, which limited their visibility. Building a website was technically daunting, and hiring a developer wasn't in the budget for most independent restaurants. When the US financial crisis struck in 2007, dining out was one of the first luxuries that families eliminated from their budgets. Corporate chains felt the effects immediately, and some closed their doors; however, for the most part, the economic impact simply meant making cutbacks until things got better.

As bleak as the crisis got, there was light at the end of the tunnel for supper clubs. Cable shows like *Mad Men* depicted the 1960s pinnacle of fine dining, drinking to excess, and chain-smoking. Viewers were inspired to go back to the restaurants

Johnnie Reynolds' sign, 2020;
illustration of the sign in its
heyday, 1974

of yesteryear to experience a bit of that "old-fashioned" lifestyle. New television
sub-channels like AntennaTV, Movies! and MeTV dished out the nostalgia of old
TV reruns and films, as if they were something new to behold. In addition, Turner
Classic Movies (TCM), Netflix, Amazon Prime, and other streaming services
offered classic movies and shows at a click of a mouse or remote. Beginning in 2011,
Wisconsin supper clubs were featured in documentaries and books, which brought
renewed attention to places that, for many, held fond memories and became a special
experience for the newcomers. Cocktails, once the main focus of the bar crowd at
a club, now gave way to a variety of imported and domestic wines and local craft
beers. Madison's Capital Brewing introduced "Supper Club" lager beer to the market
in 2010. It quickly became their second-highest selling beer. In 2016, the Wisconsin
Department of Tourism, headed by Stephanie Klett, made the state's supper clubs
the focus of their spring tourism campaign. It was one of the organization's most

Classified
advertisements,
1961 and 1978

successful efforts ever. Travel Wisconsin Supper Club concession stands opened in Madison's Kohl Center and Lambeau Field in Green Bay. August 31, 2017, was declared Supper Club Day in the state.

Today, Wisconsinites and regular visitors to the state know what to expect at a supper club. But outside of the Midwest, a supper club can look and feel quite differ-ent. Sometimes it is a pop-up dining event that features local chefs and a set menu for a limited number of invited guests. It may be a monthly, members-only supper hosted at someone's home, much like those hosted by housewives in the early-to-mid-1900s. There are high-priced supper clubs with DJs playing thumping electronic dance music (today's Wiggle Wiggle?) meant for a younger crowd. And there are the retro-loungey supper clubs, a kind of Las Vegas-style showplace, where big steaks, fancy cocktails, and entertainment from comedians, singers, variety acts, and more are featured. It can be quite confusing to identify a supper club outside of Wisconsin.

The last and possibly most egregious type, in this author's opinion, is the make-believe supper club. Here, the basic components of the Wisconsin supper club experience are cherry-picked, repackaged, and served at ridiculous prices. One example of this phenomenon, which I refer to as "Disneyfication," is the St. Clair Supper Club in Chicago. It was opened in 2019 by chef Grant Achatz and his business partner Nick Kokonas, who own several upscale restaurants in Chicago, including Alinea, Aviary, and Roister. At St. Clair, an old-fashioned will set you back $14. The three appetizers on the *à la carte* menu range from $19 to $27, and prime rib is the only meat served—and it is only served medium-rare. Prices start at $49 for a Queen cut, $57 for the King, and $83 for the St. Clair (respective weights unknown). Sides are $12 and include Yorkshire pudding and a $9 "spun" Caesar salad (all an apparent nod to Lawry's The Prime Rib). The Friday fish fry special is an eye-watering $32, and dessert is $16. No ice cream drinks are available—only pie, pudding, and tortes.

A note on the overly austere menu makes it clear that there are no vegetarian options available, illustrated by a cartoon stalk of broccoli crying behind a no symbol. Perhaps one customer, in their online review of St. Clair, already put it best: "This is the restau-rant I would create if I wanted to personally and singlehandedly poison the concept of a supper club for all eternity." Luckily, with an abundance of honest-to-goodness—and more reasonably priced—supper clubs in Wisconsin, there isn't much reason to stray.

SUPPER CLUB FIRES

Supper club fires were a common occurrence in Wisconsin, as they were usually housed in old, wooden buildings. Grease-clogged chimneys, faulty electrical wiring, carelessly tossed cigarettes, natural disasters, and even arson were often the cause. Nationally, supper club fires made world headlines with devastating fatality numbers. The 1942 Cocoanut Grove fire in Boston killed 492, and the 1977 Beverly Hills Supper Club conflagration in Kentucky left 165 dead and more than 200 wounded. While these major disasters led to stricter safety codes, the supper club blazes in Wisconsin clubs were nowhere near as deadly. In most cases, damage from a fire led to the complete rebuilding or renovation of the clubs—bigger dining rooms, a better kitchen, or a brand-new building altogether. Of course, for some, it was the permanent end to a business; for example, the Gun Club in Beloit and Shaffer's Supper Club in Crivitz never reopened after devastating fires in 2010 and 2014, respectively.

Fire at Dunkel's White Oaks, Burlington, 1985; supper club fire, Sheboygan,1993

Chapter 14

LAST CALL

As closing time approaches at the supper club, someone's at the door wanting a drink and something to eat. The bartender, who also happens to be the owner, invites them in and pours one final round for the few folks sitting at the bar. In this boozy, late night atmosphere, a relatively thoughtful discussion takes place on matters that are significant to any supper club enthusiast. With that in mind, here's one last round of topics before the end of the day.

Relish Trays

In Wisconsin, the humble relish tray has been elevated to the lofty heights of superstardom by supper club aficionados who believe that its presence is the sure sign of a legitimate supper club. At the very least, a complimentary selection of vegetables and dip is a welcome sign of good hospitality. The tradition emerged in the late 1800s when meals often began with a selection of pickled vegetables, usually olives, gherkins, or chow chow, and fresh vegetables including celery, green onions, and radishes. The veggies were something healthy to nibble on while reading the menu and deciding what size steak to order. Horseradish, anchovies, salted almonds, and pickled walnuts were also sometimes served.

As the years went by, the relish tray became an important part of dining in the Midwest, both inside and outside the home. At some Wisconsin clubs, choices were expanded to include cottage cheese, liverwurst, pickled peppers, carrots, corn salad, bean salad, pickled herring, and more. The sheer abundance of some relish trays made them a meal on their own.

Sadly, relish trays began to disappear from supper club tables in the mid-2000s and were replaced with salad bars or a simple tossed salad served with a meal. Some places opted to start charging for a relish tray as a cost-saving measure and because many customers weren't eating them as they once had. Luckily, there are still a number of supper clubs that offer complimentary relish trays, so make sure to enjoy them.

A large iced relish bowl at Leon & Eddie's, New York City, 1944

Pinewood Supper
Club, Mosinee

Pic-N-Serv olive grabber

Dobie's Steak
House, St. Francis

The 615 Club, Beloit

Oliver Hardy and
Stan Laurel in
Below Zero, 1930

Fritz Feld and Katharine Hepburn
in *Bringing Up Baby*, 1938

Hollywood Relish Trays

Relish trays have appeared in a number of Hollywood movies since the 1930s. An early example is the comedy duo Laurel and Hardy's short *Below Zero* from 1930. In it, the pair invite a policeman to have something to eat at a nearby greasy spoon. After Hardy orders "Three great big steaks, smothered in onions," he tells Laurel to "Pass the *hors d'oeuvres*"— a plate of celery and olives that was brought to the table when they sat down.

In Howard Hawks' comedy *Bringing Up Baby* from 1938, Katharine Hepburn shows psychiatrist Dr. Lehman (played by Fritz Feld) how to do a trick with olives from a relish tray on his table in the country club dining room.

The 1954 holiday classic *White Christmas* shows Bing Crosby and Danny Kaye seated at a dinner table at the Vermont lodge owned by General Waverly (played by Dean Jagger). Emma (played by Mary Wickes) delivers a huge, iced relish tray loaded with radishes, black and green olives, and celery to begin the meal. Incidentally, there are three supper clubs in *White Christmas*: Novello's in Florida, the Carousel Club in New York City, and the nightclub in the Columbia Inn in Vermont.

While they may not get top billing—or any billing at all—relish trays have had their place as some of the most mouthwatering props in movie history.

Above: Bing Crosby and Danny Kaye in *White Christmas*, 1954

Duncan Hines

any people of a certain age will remember that, before customer review sites like Yelp and TripAdvisor, word of mouth and newspaper food critics, like the *Milwaukee Journal Sentinel*'s Dennis Getto, were the primary way to find out where to enjoy a good meal. But beginning in the late 1930s, a recommendation from Duncan Hines was considered the gold standard for restaurants.

Europeans had *The Michelin Guide*, which was first published in 1900, but the US had no similar restaurant guide until Hines came along. During the 1920s, '30s, and '40s, Hines was a traveling salesman. On the road, he kept meticulous notes on where he liked to dine. At first, he shared his findings with his friends and family, but in 1936, he self-published *Adventures in Good Eating*. The guide, which he sold for a dollar, covered 475 restaurants across the US. The first printing quickly sold out. Hines, now in his fifties, had found a new career. Later, he licensed his name to a variety of products, including the well-known cake mix, ice cream, and cookware made by Regal Ware in Wisconsin.

Outside The Supper Club in Bailey's Harbor, Door County, circa 1950s

Brandy

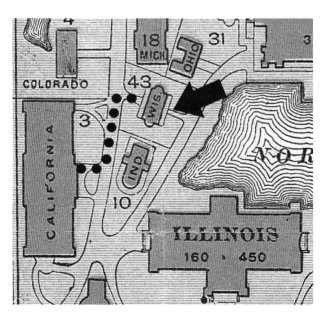

Finally, three words about brandy: Wisconsin loves it. Seriously. According to Korbel, of the 280,800 cases of brandy made in 2018, over 50 percent were sold in Wisconsin. (Sadly, the rumor that there is one large vat in the Korbel factory marked "Wisconsin" is not true.) The Korbel brothers, Joseph, Anton, and Francis, began to produce brandy at their winery in Guerneville, California, in 1889. Supposedly, they brought their products to the California Pavilion at the 1893 World's Columbian Exposition in Chicago. Wisconsin's pavilion just happened to be located near California's, so without a doubt, plenty of Wisconsinites likely wandered over to sample the brandy produced in the Golden State, whether it was by Korbel or another company. This may very well be where Wisconsin's love for brandy began.

If there was any brandy being produced in Wisconsin at the time, it was homemade and possibly made with some other fruit that is easier to grow, like apples. As a comparison, in 1907, California produced 4 million gallons of brandy. Just twelve years later, Prohibition brought an end to brandy making in California; Korbel did not resume production until the 1950s. Wisconsin's love affair with brandy—and especially brandy old-fashioneds—most likely took hold around that time. Wisconsin drinkers have had a variety of brandy producers to choose from, including Coronet, Christian Brothers, and E&J.

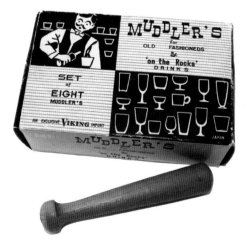

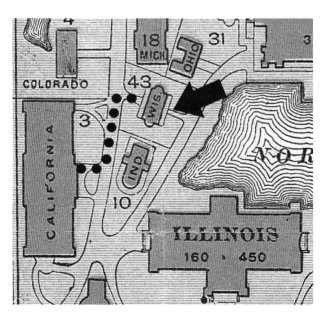

Map showing the proximity of the Wisconsin and California pavilions at the World's Columbian Exposition in Chicago, 1893

Place Your Butts Here

Smoking in bars, restaurants, and other indoor places was phased out in Wisconsin on July 5, 2010. Here are some relics of those days of yore.

Epilogue

There is no end to the history of supper clubs in Wisconsin—or elsewhere, for that matter. I am confident they will continue to be places we gather and visit for a long time.

Still, much of the writing of this book took place in 2020, during the early days of the COVID-19 pandemic. The impact on restaurants has been catastrophic, especially for those who work at family-owned establishments like supper clubs. During the crisis, I've spoken with a number of owners, as well as their customers who've visited the clubs—just not as they were able to before. I am glad to report that club owners have adapted to safety policies in order to keep customers happy and have come up with new ways of serving their fare. Among their clever innovations are old-fashioned kits, which include a bottle of brandy, old-fashioned mix, soda, and fruit; to-go meals such as buckets of fish and chicken; and other individual dinners and appetizers. In some cases, customer response was overwhelming; many purchased gift certificates and excess dishes to help their favorite supper clubs stay afloat.

In the introduction, I mentioned the moxie I believe supper club owners need in order to be successful. 2020 has been the ultimate test of that fighting spirit. As Albert Einstein once said, "In the middle of a difficulty lies opportunity." Hopefully, as you read this, the worst will be over, and we are all able to gather at our favorite supper clubs once more.

HERE'S

LOOKING

AT

YOU

THE HOFFMAN HOUSE at Madison, Wisc.

Hoffman House **ISHNALA** on Mirror Lake near Wisconsin Dells

"Enjoy a friendly welcome to superb food and natural beauty"

Acknowledgments

Thanks and a hearty elbow bump to Doug Seibold for taking a chance and giving this book series life, to Rick Kogan for his encouragement and support, and Al Zukrow for the connection. Many thanks go to Naomi Huffman, Becca James, Jane Seibold, Diana Slickman, Morgan Krehbiel, Jacqueline Jarik, and the rest of the staff at Agate Publishing for helping to make this book a reality. Muchas gracias to Fred Fischer for the excellent scans of the oversize menus and documents and a chance to grab a killer burrito. Additional thanks go to Norman Carlson, John Sidoff, Mark Eckert, Susan Vallet, Michael Volpe, Tom Volpe, Hollis Tischner, James Prinz, Kurt Koenig, R. Douglas Aungst, Dan Pagel, Paulette Horn, Ed Hoefs, Chris Wiken, Jimmy Jackson, Rev. Dale Klitzke, Rev. Paul Klitzke, Archie Ulm, Tom Shuman, Mary Bergin, the staff at the Milwaukee Public Library's Tippecanoe Branch, Bob Prosser, Steve Schaffer at the Milwaukee County Historical Society, Peter Exley at ArchitectureIsFun, Nathan Lewis at Vintage Aerial, Margie Healy at Korbel, Parker Dean, Richard N. Frank at Lawry's, Tom Dvorak and Kat Worzalla at Milwaukee Public Television, Charlene and Oswald Lettrari, and Pat McRae for his work on the Wisconsin Supper Clubs website.

Index

Starship Encounters, 73–74
Starship, 2, 74–75
Steak House 100, 151
Steak Knife Restaurant, 178
Steamship Mayflower, The, 57
Steele, George, 188
Steele, George, 88
Stiller, Jerry, 149
Stupar, Joseph, 106
Sturtevant's La Grange, 138
Sun Ra (band), 75
Sunset Gardens, 36
Supper club (definition), 8, 11–21
Supper Club Book, The, 130
Supper Club, The, 15–16, 193
Swing Seven, 60

T

T.G.I. Fridays, 182
T.S.O.L., 75
Tam O'Shanter, 8, 100
Tatum, Art, 88
Tee-Pee Supper Club, The, 118–121
Tenderloin Inn, 77
Tennyson, Alfred, 19
Tense Experts, 75
Tent, The, 33
The Ahmad Jamal Trio, 99
The Charcoal Broiled Steak House, 195
The Jazz Singer, 28
The Sheik, 165
Theiele, Adolph, 123
Theleen's Place, 33
Thelma Carleton, 26
Thiesen, T.W., 22
Thomas Healy, 26
Thompson, Allan "Ed," 120
Thompson, Artie, 120
Thompson, Juliann, 120
Thompson, Tommy, 120
Three Cellars Wine, 151
Tic Toc Club, 64
Tischendorf, Roger, 145–146
Tischendorf, Roy, 145–146
Tischendorf, Selma, 145–146
Tivoli Gardens, 172

Tomah Theatre, 118
Town House, 72
Towne Hotel, 66
Towne Room, 66, 68
Travelers Building, 154
Travelers Insurance, 156
Travelers' Inn, 33
Treasury Department, 34
Tricoli, Louis, 43
Troggs, The, 75
Tucker, Sophie, 28, 66, 99
Turk's Inn (Brooklyn), The 48
Turk's Inn (Hayward), The, 30–31, 44, 46–48
Tusa, Albert "Al," 64–66, 72
Tutankhamun, 122
Twenty-First Amendment, 23

U

Uecker, Bob, 101
Ullmer, Agnes, 115–116
Ullmer, Harold "Dutch," 113, 115–117
Ulm, Archie, 176–179
Universal Pictures, 24, 29, 171
University Club, 160
University of Wisconsin, 33, 51
Unlisted Number, 81
Urban, Clark, 53

V

Vagabonds, 96, 99
Valentino, Rudolph, 165
Vallet, Susan, 95
Valli, June, 72
Van de Kamp, 6, 8
Vanderbilt, William K., I, 15
Vanderbilt, William K., II, 19
Vanity Café, The, 65
Vassallo, Johnny, 106
Ventures, The, 75
Village Supper Club, The 139
Vinehout, Kathleen, 120
Violent Femmes, 75
Volpe, Dominic, 95
Volpe, John, 94–96, 98–99

Volstead Act, 28, 32
Volstead, Andrew, 23

W

Wagner, John, 22
Waiters Club, The, 57
Waitresses, The, 75
Warner Bros., 29
Wartime Prohibition Act, 23
Weatherly, Bruce, 79
Webb, Clifton, 28
Weber, Jean-Paul 156
Weed, Duane 120
Welch, Leo, 132
Welch's Embers, 132
White Christmas, 191
White Manor Inn, 147
White Manor, The, 77, 147
White Rock, 27, 33, 56
White Swan, The, 33
White, Stanford, 15, 18
Wickes, Mary, 191
Wiken, Keith, 116
Willard, Fred, 149
Williams, Andy, 99
Williams, Billy, 99
Winard, Jeff, 173–174
Winchell, Walter, 59, 166
Wisconsin Department of Tourism, 183
Wisconsin State Fair, 150
Wolf River Community Bank, 108
World Series, 40
World's Columbian Exposition of 1893, 194
WTMJ Radio, 168

X

X, 75
XCleavers, 75

Y

Yankovic, Frankie, 173–174
Yorkshire pudding, 8, 184
Young Rascals, 178

ABOUT THE AUTHOR

RON FAIOLA has been called "Wisconsin's legacy film-maker" and a "supper club guru." His best-selling book series, *Wisconsin Supper Clubs: An Old-Fashioned Experience* (2013), and *Wisconsin Supper Clubs: Another Round* (2016), helped ignite supper club fever in the Badger State. His many years of supper club research led to his third book, *The Wisconsin Supper Clubs Story: An Illustrated History With Relish*.

Faiola is an author and photographer. His documentary films about popular Dairyland topics such as fish frys, church festivals and supper clubs have appeared on PBS stations nationwide. He has earned mentions in the *New York Times*, *Chicago Tribune*, *USA Today* and *Milwaukee Journal Sentinel* and has been interviewed by WGN's Rick Kogan, Milk Street's Christopher Kimball and travel expert Rudy Maxa.

Faiola is a drummer and a former founding member of the Milwaukee punk rock band Couch Flambeau. He resides in a "Greendale Original" in the historic Village of Greendale.

For his list of over 250 supper clubs in Wisconsin, visit: WisconsinSupperClubs.com.

NITE-OWL
SUPPER CLUB

the COACHMAN
Supper Club

BALDWIN, WISCONSIN

Supper
Club

"At the De
Fischer
Supper

LAKE DELTON,

call Janesville
PL. 2-5437

Cavi's
supper club
and lounge

halfway between
Beloit - Janesville
on highway 51

CLOSE COVER

FOR SAFETY - STRIKE ON BACK*

the Coachman
SUPPER CLUB
BALDWIN
WIS.

WHEELER'S
Supper Club

CIRCUS
SUPPER CLUB
205 N. 3RD - LA CROSSE, WIS.

Dug Out
Supper Club
DICKEYVILLE, WIS.

HWY. 35 & 61

(10 MILES FROM
DUBUQUE, IOWA)

Poole's Supper

Route 42
The
BREAK
RACINE

Known for FINE

SEA FOOD
STEAKS
CHOPS
CHICKEN

fine foods
LOUIE'S
SUPPER
CLUB

On the
Sup

Limestone
Castle
Supper Club
Hwy. 29 3 miles
East of

Good Food
is
Good
Health

Wi
SUPPE
CEDAR